I0003401

Understanding RAID: Data Protection and Performance in Storage Systems

James Relington

Copyright © 2025 James Relington

All rights reserved

DEDICATION

To those who seek knowledge, inspiration, and new perspectives—
may this book be a companion on your journey, a spark for curiosity,
and a reminder that every page turned is a step toward discovery.

AKNOWLEDGEMENTS

I would like to express my deepest gratitude to everyone who contributed to the creation of this book. To my colleagues and mentors, your insights and expertise have been invaluable. A special thank you to my family and friends for their unwavering support and encouragement throughout this journey.

Introduction to RAID: A Comprehensive Overview

RAID, which stands for Redundant Array of Independent Disks, is a technology used to combine multiple hard drives or solid-state drives (SSDs) into a single logical unit, improving data storage efficiency, redundancy, and performance. Over time, RAID has become an essential part of data storage strategies, offering significant benefits to both home users and enterprise environments. The technology allows for the management of several hard drives or SSDs as one cohesive storage unit, thereby providing increased fault tolerance and faster access speeds. RAID's primary function is to protect data against hardware failures while optimizing read and write operations.

The concept of RAID emerged during the late 1980s when the need for more reliable and faster data storage solutions became apparent. At that time, traditional disk storage systems, while effective, often suffered from performance bottlenecks and lacked redundancy mechanisms to prevent data loss in the event of a hardware failure. Researchers at the University of California, Berkeley, developed the original RAID model, aiming to address these shortcomings by integrating multiple drives into a unified system. Initially, RAID was a solution for high-end servers and workstations, but over the years, its application spread to more mainstream consumer and enterprise systems, making it an indispensable part of modern data management.

RAID technology works by dividing data into smaller chunks and distributing these chunks across multiple drives in a way that either increases performance, provides fault tolerance, or combines both. The configuration of the drives, or the RAID level, determines how the data is distributed and whether redundancy is provided. There are several different RAID levels, each offering distinct advantages in terms of speed, redundancy, and capacity. For example, RAID 0 is focused on performance and speed by striping data across multiple drives without any redundancy. On the other hand, RAID 1 mirrors data across two drives, offering a higher level of data protection but without a significant boost in performance.

One of the most important benefits of RAID is its ability to offer fault tolerance. In a typical non-RAID setup, if a hard drive fails, the data on that drive is lost, and the system may become inoperable until the drive is replaced and the data is recovered. RAID, however, can protect against this risk by storing redundant copies of the data across multiple drives. If one drive fails, the data can be recovered from another drive in the array, ensuring that the system remains operational. This is particularly important for businesses and enterprises that rely on constant uptime and cannot afford to lose critical data. RAID levels such as RAID 5 and RAID 6, which use parity data to reconstruct lost information, offer high levels of fault tolerance with minimal impact on storage capacity.

In addition to fault tolerance, RAID also provides performance benefits. When multiple drives are used in parallel, data can be read or written simultaneously, leading to significant improvements in access speeds. RAID 0, for example, increases performance by striping data across multiple drives, allowing for faster read and write operations since multiple drives can be accessed concurrently. RAID 10, which combines both mirroring and striping, offers both increased performance and redundancy, making it a popular choice for environments that require both speed and reliability.

Another key advantage of RAID is its scalability. As storage needs grow, RAID configurations can be expanded by adding more drives to the array. This scalability allows businesses and individuals to increase their storage capacity without the need to replace existing drives or rebuild their entire system. Depending on the RAID level and the specific setup, adding additional drives can improve performance or enhance fault tolerance, making RAID an adaptable solution for evolving data storage needs.

RAID is commonly used in both consumer-grade and enterprise-grade storage solutions. In personal computing, users often implement RAID to improve the speed of their storage systems or to ensure that their data is protected against drive failure. Many modern consumer-grade computers come with RAID support built into the motherboard or via software solutions, allowing users to easily configure their systems for optimal performance. In enterprise environments, RAID is used extensively in data centers, cloud storage solutions, and network-attached storage (NAS) systems, where high availability and redundancy are critical. Large-scale businesses rely on RAID to store vast amounts of data across multiple drives, ensuring both security and reliability.

Despite its many advantages, RAID does have its limitations. One of the primary concerns with RAID is the potential for data loss due to human error or controller failure. While RAID provides fault tolerance against individual drive failures, it is not immune to other forms of data loss, such as accidental deletion or corruption of data. RAID systems also require careful monitoring and maintenance to ensure that drives are functioning properly. When a drive fails in a RAID array, it is crucial to replace the drive promptly to prevent data loss or performance degradation. Additionally, RAID can be expensive, especially in enterprise environments where multiple high-capacity drives are needed to support large storage needs.

RAID is often confused with backup, but it is important to note that RAID is not a substitute for proper backup practices. While RAID provides redundancy, it is not designed to protect against all types of data loss, such as corruption, malware, or accidental deletion. A comprehensive backup strategy, including off-site or cloud backups, is still necessary to ensure complete data protection.

In conclusion, RAID remains one of the most effective and widely used technologies for improving data protection and performance in modern storage systems. Whether in home computers, small businesses, or large enterprises, RAID provides a versatile solution for managing and safeguarding data. Understanding the different RAID levels and how they function is essential for anyone looking to optimize their storage system. As data continues to grow and the need for faster, more reliable storage solutions increases, RAID will continue to play a critical role in the evolution of data storage technologies.

The Evolution of Data Storage Technologies

Data storage technologies have undergone a profound transformation over the years, evolving from early manual methods to sophisticated digital systems capable of handling vast amounts of information. The journey of data storage development spans several decades, reflecting the rapid advancements in computing technology and the growing need for more efficient and reliable ways to store, retrieve, and protect data. Understanding the evolution of data storage not only provides insight into the history of computing but also helps to contextualize the current and future trends in storage solutions.

In the early days of computing, data storage was a relatively simple and manual process. The first computers, such as the ENIAC and UNIVAC, used punched cards to store data. These cards were a physical representation of data, with holes punched in specific patterns to represent information. While effective for the time, punched cards had several limitations, including a relatively low data storage capacity and a cumbersome process for input and retrieval. Despite these drawbacks, punched cards were a staple of early computing systems, used extensively for data entry, programming, and processing tasks.

As technology advanced, magnetic storage emerged as a more efficient and practical solution for storing data. The first significant breakthrough came in the 1950s with the introduction of magnetic tape drives. Magnetic tape offered much greater storage capacity than punched cards, allowing data to be stored in a continuous strip of tape coated with a magnetic material. This innovation enabled more efficient storage and retrieval of data, making it suitable for larger-scale computing environments. Magnetic tape was primarily used for batch processing and backup purposes, but it quickly became an essential tool for data storage in both commercial and scientific applications.

The next significant leap in data storage technology came with the invention of the hard disk drive (HDD) in the 1960s. The first hard drives were large, cumbersome devices that were used primarily by mainframe computers. Unlike magnetic tape, which relied on sequential access, hard drives provided random access to data, allowing for much faster retrieval. The hard disk drive represented a monumental shift in data storage, as it made it possible to access and modify data more quickly and efficiently than ever before. Early HDDs were expensive and had limited storage capacities, but they laid the foundation for the modern data storage systems we use today.

As computing technology continued to advance, storage capacities grew exponentially, and the need for more sophisticated data management solutions became apparent. The 1980s saw the emergence of new storage technologies, such as optical disk drives and floppy disks. Optical disks, such as CDs and later DVDs, offered a way to store data in a non-volatile, compact format that was easy to distribute. Floppy disks, although limited in capacity, became widely used for data transfer and backup purposes. These technologies allowed users to store and share data more easily than with earlier methods, marking a significant step forward in the accessibility and portability of data storage.

The 1990s and early 2000s saw the proliferation of personal computers and the rise of consumer-driven data storage technologies. One of the most significant developments during this time was the introduction of the CD-ROM, which revolutionized data distribution and software installation. The ability to store hundreds of megabytes of data on a single optical disc made it possible to deliver software, games, and multimedia content to a mass market. At the same time, the floppy disk began to fade into obsolescence, replaced by the more versatile and higher-capacity CD-ROMs. As personal computers became more powerful, the need for faster and more efficient storage solutions increased, leading to the development of newer technologies like digital versatile discs (DVDs) and Blu-ray discs.

Simultaneously, advancements in hard drive technology continued to push the boundaries of data storage. The capacity of hard drives increased dramatically, and by the early 2000s, hard disk drives with storage capacities of hundreds of gigabytes became commonplace in personal computers. With this surge in storage capacity came a demand for faster access speeds, leading to the development of technologies like Serial ATA (SATA) and Serial Attached SCSI (SAS). These interfaces allowed for faster data transfer rates and improved performance, making it possible for users to store and access large amounts of data quickly and efficiently.

The most recent wave of data storage innovation has been driven by the rise of solid-state drives (SSDs). Unlike traditional hard disk drives, which rely on spinning magnetic platters to read and write data, SSDs use flash memory to store data electronically. This shift to solid-state technology has had a profound impact on data storage performance. SSDs offer much faster read and write speeds compared to HDDs, making them ideal for applications that require high-speed data access, such as gaming, video editing, and data analytics. The advent of SSDs has also led to the development of new storage form factors, such as NVMe (Non-Volatile Memory Express), which further increases data transfer speeds and reduces latency.

In parallel with the development of individual storage devices, the need for large-scale, networked storage solutions has become increasingly important. As organizations have grown and data volumes have surged, traditional local storage systems have struggled to meet the demands of enterprise environments. This has led to the development of network-attached storage (NAS) and storage area networks (SANs). These systems allow organizations to centralize their data storage in a single, easily accessible location while providing the flexibility to scale storage capacity as needed. Both NAS and SANs provide advanced data management features, including redundancy, backup, and remote access, making them essential tools for modern enterprises.

The advent of cloud storage has further transformed the way data is stored and managed. Cloud storage solutions, such as Google Drive, Dropbox, and Amazon Web Services (AWS), have made it possible for individuals and businesses to store vast amounts of data remotely, without the need to maintain physical storage devices. Cloud storage has been driven by the increasing availability of high-speed internet connections and the growing need for scalable, on-demand storage solutions. The cloud has introduced new concepts of data availability, disaster recovery, and collaboration, allowing users to access their data from virtually anywhere in the world.

The evolution of data storage technologies has been marked by a continual drive for greater speed, capacity, and reliability. From the early days of punched cards and magnetic tape to the rise of solid-state drives and cloud storage, each new innovation has played a crucial role in meeting the growing demands of the digital age. As the volume of data continues to increase, the evolution of data storage technologies will undoubtedly continue, with new advancements on the horizon that will further enhance the efficiency, security, and accessibility of data storage solutions.

Basic Concepts in RAID

RAID, which stands for Redundant Array of Independent Disks, is a data storage technology that combines multiple physical drives into a single logical unit to improve performance, increase storage capacity, and provide fault tolerance. The primary goal of RAID is to enhance data reliability and provide protection against hardware failure while optimizing storage efficiency and access speed. RAID works by distributing data across multiple drives, with different configurations depending on the desired balance between redundancy and performance. Understanding the fundamental concepts of RAID is essential for anyone seeking to build, manage, or troubleshoot data storage systems.

At the heart of RAID technology lies the concept of combining several storage devices into a single array. When multiple drives are used together, data is distributed in such a way that either redundancy or performance enhancements are achieved, or both. Redundancy in RAID is achieved by creating copies of data or using error correction mechanisms that allow for the recovery of lost data in the event of a drive failure. This is particularly important in enterprise environments where system downtime and data loss can have serious financial and operational consequences. Performance, on the other hand, is enhanced by distributing data across several drives, allowing for faster read and write operations. Depending on the specific RAID configuration, these two objectives—data protection and performance—can be optimized in different ways.

RAID levels, or the different configurations within RAID, define how data is distributed and how redundancy is achieved. Each RAID level has its own strengths and weaknesses in terms of performance, redundancy, and storage efficiency. The simplest RAID level is RAID 0, which stripes data across multiple drives without any redundancy. While RAID 0 offers improved performance by allowing data to be read and written to multiple drives simultaneously, it does not provide any fault tolerance. This means that if one drive in a RAID 0 array fails, all data is lost. Despite this risk, RAID 0 is often used in applications where speed is paramount, and data loss is either not a concern or can be mitigated by other means, such as regular backups.

RAID 1, in contrast, offers redundancy by mirroring data across two drives. This means that each drive in the RAID 1 array contains an exact copy of the data. If one drive fails, the other drive still contains a complete copy of the data, allowing for recovery without data loss. While RAID 1 provides fault tolerance, it does so at the cost of storage efficiency, as the data is effectively duplicated. RAID 1 is commonly used in situations where data protection is more important than maximizing storage capacity, such as in personal computers or small business environments where data loss could be catastrophic.

RAID 5 is one of the most widely used configurations, combining both redundancy and performance. It requires a minimum of three drives and uses a technique called parity to provide fault tolerance. In a RAID 5 array, data is striped across multiple drives, and parity information is distributed among the drives. Parity acts as a form of error correction, enabling the array to recover lost data if one drive fails. This makes RAID 5 a popular choice for enterprise environments where high availability and data protection are crucial. While RAID 5 offers a good balance between performance, redundancy, and storage efficiency, it is important to note that it is vulnerable to data loss if two drives fail simultaneously. To mitigate this risk, many enterprises use RAID 5 in combination with regular backups and monitoring systems.

RAID 6 is similar to RAID 5 but offers an additional layer of redundancy. It requires a minimum of four drives and uses two sets of parity data, which provides protection against the failure of two drives. This additional redundancy makes RAID 6 a more reliable choice for environments where uptime and data integrity are critical. However, this extra protection comes at a cost in terms of both performance and storage efficiency. The increased number of parity calculations can slow down read and write operations, and the additional parity data reduces the total usable storage capacity. Despite these trade-offs, RAID 6 is often used in high-availability environments such as data centers and cloud storage systems where data protection is a top priority.

RAID 10, sometimes referred to as RAID 1+0, combines the benefits of both RAID 1 and RAID 0. It requires a minimum of four drives and uses both mirroring and striping. Data is mirrored across pairs of drives, and then those mirrored pairs are striped together. This configuration offers both fault tolerance and improved performance, making RAID 10 a popular choice for applications that require high-speed data access and redundancy, such as databases or high-performance computing systems. While RAID 10 offers excellent performance and redundancy, it also requires twice the number of drives as RAID 5 or RAID 6 to achieve the same amount of usable storage. As a result, it may not be the most storage-efficient option for all environments.

The concept of hot spares is another important aspect of RAID technology. A hot spare is an additional, unused drive that is included in the RAID array to automatically replace a failed drive. When a drive fails, the RAID array will use the hot spare to rebuild the lost data, ensuring that the system continues to function without interruption. Hot spares are commonly used in enterprise environments where maintaining uptime is critical, and they help to ensure that data remains available even in the event of a hardware failure.

RAID can be implemented in two ways: hardware RAID and software RAID. Hardware RAID uses a dedicated RAID controller card that manages the array and offloads the processing of RAID tasks from the system's main processor. This allows for better performance and often includes advanced features such as battery-backed cache and the ability to manage larger arrays. Software RAID, on the other hand, is implemented through the operating system and does not require dedicated hardware. While software RAID is generally less expensive, it may not offer the same level of performance or advanced features as hardware RAID. Software RAID is typically used in smaller systems or in situations where cost is a concern.

One of the challenges with RAID is the process of rebuilding a failed drive. When a drive fails in a RAID array, the system must reconstruct the lost data using the parity information or mirrored copies on the remaining drives. This process can be time-consuming, especially in larger arrays, and can put additional strain on the remaining drives. As a result, it is essential to monitor RAID arrays carefully and replace failed drives promptly to prevent further issues.

RAID is a powerful technology that has become essential in modern data storage systems. It enables organizations to achieve a balance between performance, redundancy, and storage capacity. While each RAID level has its own advantages and trade-offs, understanding the basic concepts behind RAID is critical for anyone involved in the management or maintenance of data storage systems. The flexibility of RAID makes it an invaluable tool for a wide range of applications, from personal computers to large-scale enterprise environments, where data protection, reliability, and speed are paramount.

The Role of RAID in Data Protection

Data protection is one of the most critical aspects of managing a storage system, especially in today's digital age where the volume of data generated and processed is growing exponentially. With data being a fundamental asset for businesses, governments, and individuals, ensuring its integrity, availability, and security is paramount. RAID, or Redundant Array of Independent Disks, plays a significant role in data protection by offering a range of solutions to safeguard data against hardware failure, which is one of the most common causes of data loss. By using multiple disk drives in various configurations, RAID allows for improved reliability, fault tolerance, and data recovery, making it an essential technology for protecting critical information.

The core principle behind RAID is redundancy. In traditional single-disk storage systems, the failure of a disk typically results in the complete loss of data stored on that disk. This creates a significant risk, particularly for businesses where data loss can lead to operational disruption, financial losses, and reputational damage. RAID addresses this issue by distributing data across multiple disks, ensuring that if one disk fails, the data is still accessible from another disk within the array. The level of redundancy varies depending on the RAID level chosen, but in every case, RAID aims to ensure that the failure of one or more disks does not lead to data loss.

One of the simplest and most effective ways RAID achieves data protection is through mirroring. RAID 1, for example, mirrors data across two drives. This means that each drive in the RAID 1 array contains an identical copy of the data. If one drive fails, the other drive continues to function, providing uninterrupted access to the data. This redundancy makes RAID 1 an excellent choice for environments where data availability is crucial, such as in small businesses or personal computing systems. While RAID 1 provides excellent protection against single-drive failures, it comes at the cost of storage efficiency, as the data is essentially duplicated across both drives.

In addition to mirroring, RAID uses parity to achieve data protection. Parity is a form of error-checking information that is distributed across multiple drives in the array. In RAID 5, for example, data is striped across three or more drives, and parity information is distributed among the drives as well. Parity allows the system to rebuild the data of a failed drive by using the information stored on the remaining drives. This method provides fault tolerance while maintaining better storage efficiency compared to RAID 1, as the total storage capacity of the array is not halved. RAID 5 is commonly used in enterprise environments where a balance between data protection, storage capacity, and performance is necessary.

RAID 6 takes the concept of parity even further by storing two sets of parity information across the drives in the array. This provides an additional layer of protection, as it can tolerate the failure of two drives simultaneously without data loss. RAID 6 is particularly valuable in mission-critical environments where the risk of multiple drive failures is a concern, such as in large-scale data centers or cloud storage systems. While RAID 6 provides enhanced protection, it comes with a trade-off in terms of performance. The additional parity calculations can slow down read and write speeds, which may impact overall system performance. However, the benefit of being able to survive two drive failures without data loss often outweighs the performance cost, especially in systems where data availability is the highest priority.

One of the key advantages of RAID in data protection is its ability to facilitate data recovery. When a drive fails in a RAID array, the system can use the redundancy mechanisms built into the array—whether through mirroring or parity—to reconstruct the lost data. This process is known as rebuilding. In a RAID 1 setup, for example, the data from the surviving drive can be used to restore the lost data onto a new drive. In RAID 5 or RAID 6, the missing data can be reconstructed using the parity information stored on the remaining drives. This means that, in most cases, a RAID array can continue functioning normally even while a drive is being replaced, minimizing downtime and reducing the risk of data loss.

RAID also plays a critical role in protecting against the long-term risk of data degradation. Over time, disks can experience wear and tear, leading to the gradual deterioration of the data stored on them. RAID arrays help mitigate this risk by ensuring that multiple copies of the data exist on different drives. This redundancy can reduce the likelihood of data corruption going undetected and allows for more frequent checks and repairs of data integrity. Additionally, RAID can be paired with other technologies such as error-correcting codes (ECC) and regular disk health monitoring to further protect against data degradation and silent corruption.

Despite its advantages, RAID is not foolproof, and its effectiveness in protecting data is dependent on several factors, including the RAID level chosen, the configuration of the array, and the overall health of the individual drives. RAID is designed to protect against drive failures, but it does not protect against other types of data loss, such as accidental deletion, data corruption caused by software bugs, or damage due to cyberattacks like ransomware. Therefore, RAID should be viewed as a part of a broader data protection strategy that includes regular backups, data encryption, and robust cybersecurity measures.

RAID can also be used in conjunction with hot spares, which are additional, unused drives that are automatically deployed in the event of a drive failure. This ensures that the RAID array remains operational while the failed drive is replaced and rebuilt. Hot spares reduce the time needed to restore full redundancy in the array, thus improving the overall resilience of the storage system. By incorporating hot spares into a RAID configuration, organizations can minimize the risk of data loss and downtime during the rebuilding process.

Another important consideration when using RAID for data protection is the process of drive replacement. While RAID provides redundancy, it is important to replace failed drives as soon as possible to maintain the integrity of the array. If a drive fails and is not promptly replaced, the RAID array will be left vulnerable to further failures, potentially leading to data loss. Furthermore, rebuilding a RAID array after a drive failure can be a resource-intensive process that places a significant load on the remaining drives. Therefore, monitoring the health of drives in a RAID array and replacing them at the first sign of failure is crucial for maintaining data protection.

RAID is a powerful and flexible technology that plays a critical role in ensuring data protection. By using various methods of redundancy, including mirroring and parity, RAID helps safeguard data against the risk of drive failure and enables quick recovery in the event of hardware issues. While RAID is not a substitute for comprehensive data protection strategies, such as regular backups and cybersecurity measures, it remains an essential tool for organizations seeking to maintain high levels of data availability and minimize the impact of hardware failures on their operations. The role of RAID in data protection cannot be overstated, as it continues to be a key component in the design of resilient, reliable storage systems across a wide range of industries.

Understanding Storage Performance Metrics

In the world of data storage, performance is a critical factor that influences the efficiency of any storage system. Whether it is for personal use, enterprise applications, or high-performance computing environments, understanding the performance of storage systems is essential for making informed decisions about technology choices. Storage performance is determined by a combination of several metrics, each of which provides insight into the speed, responsiveness, and overall effectiveness of the system. To fully comprehend how well a storage system performs, one must consider a variety of metrics that reflect different aspects of storage, from the speed of data access to the reliability of long-term performance.

One of the primary metrics for evaluating storage performance is throughput, often referred to as bandwidth. Throughput measures the amount of data that can be transferred from the storage device to the system or from the system to the storage device within a given time frame, typically expressed in megabytes per second (MB/s) or gigabytes per second (GB/s). This metric is important for understanding how much data can be read from or written to the storage system in a particular period. For instance, in applications that involve large data sets, such as video editing or data analytics, high throughput is essential to ensure that the system can handle large file transfers without significant delays. The greater the throughput, the more data can be handled at once, reducing bottlenecks and improving overall performance.

Another crucial performance metric is latency, which refers to the delay between requesting data and receiving it. Latency is typically measured in milliseconds (ms) and represents the time it takes for the storage system to respond to a request. High latency can significantly degrade the performance of a system, as it introduces delays between user actions or application requests and the system's responses. In environments where real-time or near-real-time data processing is required, such as financial trading systems or live video streaming, low latency is a critical factor. Reducing latency is often achieved by using faster storage technologies, such as solid-state drives (SSDs), which have lower latency compared to traditional hard disk drives (HDDs). Understanding and optimizing latency is essential for ensuring smooth user experiences and efficient application performance.

IOPS, or Input/Output Operations Per Second, is another key metric in evaluating storage performance. IOPS measures the number of read and write operations that a storage system can perform in one second. This metric is particularly relevant in environments where the system handles numerous small read and write requests, such as in database management systems or virtualized environments. High IOPS is essential in these scenarios, as it indicates that the storage system can process a high volume of operations quickly. The number of IOPS that a storage system can achieve is influenced by several factors, including the type of storage medium used (SSD vs. HDD), the RAID configuration, and the interface speed. For example, an enterprise-grade SSD with a high IOPS rating is often preferred in applications requiring frequent access to small data blocks, while HDDs may suffice for sequential data access tasks, where IOPS are less important.

Beyond these core metrics, it is also important to consider the overall scalability of a storage system, which refers to its ability to handle increasing amounts of data or growing demands on performance. Scalability is crucial for businesses that expect their storage needs to grow over time. A scalable storage solution ensures that performance can be maintained or even improved as additional storage devices are added to the system. This can be achieved through various means, such as adding more drives in a RAID array, expanding the capacity of cloud storage, or upgrading to faster storage interfaces. Scalability is particularly important in cloud storage solutions, where the storage infrastructure must be able to accommodate growing data without sacrificing performance.

Another metric that impacts storage performance is the throughput-to-latency ratio. This ratio provides a more holistic view of performance by considering both how much data can be transferred and how quickly that data is accessed. A high throughput-to-latency ratio indicates that data can be transferred efficiently without significant delays. This ratio is particularly important in storage systems used for high-performance computing or applications that require both large data transfers and fast access times. A balanced throughput-to-latency ratio ensures that the system can handle heavy workloads without bottlenecks, making it ideal for environments where both speed and capacity are crucial.

Reliability and endurance are also vital considerations when assessing storage performance, especially in environments where data integrity is paramount. Reliability refers to the ability of a storage system to function without failure over a given period, while endurance is the ability of a storage device, particularly SSDs, to withstand repeated read and write operations. For example, SSDs are typically rated by their write endurance, which is often measured in terabytes written (TBW). This metric reflects the total amount of data that can be written to the drive before it begins to degrade. In high-performance environments where storage devices are subjected to constant use, understanding and monitoring the reliability and endurance of storage devices is critical to prevent data loss or system downtime.

Another important aspect of storage performance is data availability, which refers to the percentage of time that the storage system is operational and accessible. High availability is especially important for enterprise-level storage systems, where even small periods of downtime can lead to significant disruptions in business operations. RAID configurations, such as RAID 5 and RAID 6, are often used to enhance data availability by ensuring that data is protected against the failure of one or more drives. High-availability systems often incorporate redundant components, such as power supplies and network connections, to further minimize the risk of downtime.

The performance of a storage system can also be influenced by factors such as the storage interface, the protocol used for data transfer, and the type of file system implemented. Modern storage systems often use high-speed interfaces, such as Serial ATA (SATA), Serial Attached SCSI (SAS), or Non-Volatile Memory Express (NVMe), to achieve faster data transfer speeds. The protocol used for data transfer also plays a significant role in performance. For example, Fibre Channel is often used in enterprise environments for high-speed data transfers, while network-attached storage (NAS) and storage area networks (SAN) are commonly used for sharing data across multiple systems.

In the context of large-scale enterprise storage systems, the use of data tiering can further optimize performance. Data tiering involves classifying data based on its frequency of access and moving it to different storage media based on performance requirements. Frequently accessed data can be stored on high-performance SSDs, while less frequently accessed data can be stored on lower-cost, higher-capacity HDDs. This approach ensures that the storage system remains cost-effective while maintaining high performance for critical data.

Ultimately, understanding storage performance metrics is crucial for making informed decisions about storage system design, optimization, and management. By evaluating throughput, latency, IOPS, scalability, reliability, and other key factors, businesses and individuals can ensure that their storage solutions meet their specific needs for performance and efficiency. Whether for personal use, enterprise applications, or high-performance computing, the performance of a storage system can significantly impact the effectiveness of data management and access, making it essential to consider these metrics when selecting and configuring storage technologies.

RAID 0: Striping for Speed

RAID 0, often referred to as striping, is one of the simplest and most performance-focused configurations within the RAID technology spectrum. Unlike other RAID levels that prioritize redundancy and fault tolerance, RAID 0 is designed specifically to increase data throughput and overall speed by distributing data across multiple drives. This approach provides a performance boost by allowing simultaneous read and write operations on multiple disks, resulting in faster access to data. RAID 0 is commonly used in environments where performance is critical, and the risk of data loss due to disk failure is either manageable or not a primary concern.

The core concept of RAID 0 is the striping of data, which involves dividing the data into small chunks and spreading it across two or more drives. These chunks are then written and read in parallel, effectively increasing the system's throughput. The number of drives in a RAID 0 array directly impacts the overall speed, as adding more disks allows for more data to be processed simultaneously. This striping process is what differentiates RAID 0 from other RAID levels like RAID 1 or RAID 5, which focus on redundancy and data protection rather than pure performance.

Because RAID 0 does not include any form of redundancy, it offers no protection against data loss. If a single drive in the array fails, all data stored in the array is lost, as the data is split across multiple disks without any mirroring or parity. This makes RAID 0 a high-risk option for critical data storage. However, for applications where speed is the top priority and data loss is either not an issue or can be mitigated by other means, such as frequent backups or data replication, RAID 0 is an appealing choice. It is commonly used in scenarios like video editing, gaming, and high-performance computing, where large amounts of data need to be processed quickly, and the performance benefit outweighs the risk of potential data loss.

One of the most notable advantages of RAID 0 is its ability to maximize disk throughput. By striping data across multiple disks, the array can perform read and write operations concurrently. This parallelism leads to a significant performance increase, especially in applications that involve large data transfers or frequent access to data. For example, in video editing, where large video files must be accessed quickly, RAID 0 can drastically reduce loading times and improve workflow efficiency. The performance improvements are most noticeable in tasks that involve sequential data access, as the system can read or write large blocks of data across multiple drives simultaneously.

RAID 0 can also improve system responsiveness in applications that require fast access to smaller pieces of data. In these cases, the ability to read data from multiple disks at the same time can reduce bottlenecks and provide a more fluid user experience. While RAID 0 does not provide the same level of fault tolerance as other RAID configurations, its performance advantages make it an attractive option in use cases where data protection is less of a concern. It is also worth noting that the performance gains achieved with RAID 0 are not just limited to high-end systems; even in consumer-grade systems, the benefits of increased speed are noticeable, particularly in tasks like booting up the operating system or loading applications.

However, RAID 0 is not without its drawbacks. The lack of redundancy is a significant disadvantage, particularly in environments where data integrity is paramount. A single drive failure can result in the loss of all data on the array, and there is no automatic recovery process in place. For organizations or individuals who rely on the data stored in a RAID 0 array, the risk of data loss may be unacceptable. While RAID 0 can be suitable for temporary storage or non-critical applications, it should not be used as the sole storage solution for important data. Users who choose RAID 0 must be aware of the inherent risks and take appropriate precautions, such as regular backups or using additional data protection methods outside the RAID array itself.

Another consideration when using RAID 0 is the impact of drive failure on system performance. When a drive fails, the RAID 0 array loses its ability to function as intended. Since there is no redundancy in the configuration, the entire array becomes inoperable until the failed drive is replaced and the data is restored from a backup. This downtime can be a significant issue in environments that require continuous availability, such as data centers or high-performance computing systems. Moreover, the rebuilding process for a RAID 0 array is more complex than with other RAID levels, as the data needs to be reconstructed from a backup or other sources.

Despite these limitations, RAID 0 can be a highly effective solution for scenarios where performance is the top priority. The simplicity of its design, combined with its ability to provide significant performance improvements, makes it a popular choice for applications such as gaming, video production, and scientific research, where speed is critical and the risk of data loss can be managed through other means. In fact, many modern gaming systems and high-end workstations use RAID 0 arrays to provide the fast read and write speeds required for intensive workloads.

RAID 0's simplicity is another reason why it is often preferred in situations where performance is more important than redundancy. Unlike other RAID levels that require complex parity calculations or mirroring processes, RAID 0 is easy to configure and offers immediate performance benefits. This makes it an attractive option for individuals or businesses that need to optimize storage performance without dealing with the overhead of managing more complicated RAID setups.

Furthermore, RAID 0 is often used in combination with other RAID levels to achieve a balance between performance and redundancy. For example, RAID 10, also known as RAID 1+0, combines the striping of RAID 0 with the mirroring of RAID 1. This provides both the speed benefits of RAID 0 and the redundancy of RAID 1, making it an ideal choice for environments that require both high performance and data protection. However, RAID 10 requires at least four drives, whereas RAID 0 can function with as few as two drives, making RAID 0 a more cost-effective option for those who need a performance boost but do not require redundancy.

In conclusion, RAID 0 is a highly effective storage solution for users and applications that prioritize speed over data redundancy. Its ability to strip data across multiple drives allows for significant improvements in throughput, making it ideal for performance-intensive tasks. However, users must be aware of the risks associated with RAID 0, particularly the lack of data protection. For those willing to accept the risk of data loss, RAID 0 offers a cost-effective and high-performance solution.

RAID 1: Mirroring for Redundancy

RAID 1, commonly known as mirroring, is a data storage configuration designed with redundancy at its core. The primary goal of RAID 1 is to protect against data loss by creating an identical copy, or mirror, of the data on two or more disks. This redundancy ensures that if one drive fails, the data remains accessible from the other drive. RAID 1 is one of the simplest and most effective RAID levels for providing fault tolerance, making it an ideal choice for environments where data protection is a high priority and where system uptime is critical. Unlike other RAID configurations that aim to balance redundancy with performance, RAID 1 focuses solely on preserving data integrity by maintaining identical copies of the data across multiple drives.

In a RAID 1 array, data is written simultaneously to two or more drives. When a file is saved to one drive, it is automatically replicated onto the second drive, ensuring that both drives contain an exact copy of the same data. This mirroring process provides a high level of redundancy, as both drives are exact replicas of each other. If one drive fails, the system can continue to operate normally, as the second drive still holds a complete copy of the data. The failed drive can then be replaced, and the data from the surviving drive can be used to rebuild the mirror, ensuring minimal downtime and data loss.

RAID 1's design is particularly beneficial in environments where data availability is critical. For businesses or individuals relying on the continuous availability of data, RAID 1 offers a straightforward and reliable solution for minimizing the risk of data loss due to hardware failure. Whether it is financial records, customer databases, or essential business applications, RAID 1 ensures that the most critical data is always available, even in the event of a drive failure. This makes RAID 1 an excellent choice for small to medium-sized businesses, as well as personal computers where data integrity is important but the need for extreme performance is not as high.

One of the primary advantages of RAID 1 is its simplicity. Unlike other RAID levels, which can be complex due to the need for parity calculations or the distribution of data across multiple drives, RAID 1 operates on a relatively straightforward principle: duplicate the data. As a result, it is easier to implement and maintain, particularly for users who may not be as familiar with complex RAID configurations. The simplicity of RAID 1 makes it an accessible solution for both consumers and small businesses looking to protect their data without requiring extensive technical knowledge.

The redundancy provided by RAID 1 ensures that even if one drive fails, the data remains safe and accessible. This is a crucial feature for environments where uptime is important, such as web servers, email systems, or file servers. RAID 1 helps prevent data outages and downtime by offering immediate failover protection. When a drive fails, the system will continue to function as normal, with the second drive handling all read and write operations. The failed drive can be replaced with a new one, and the data from the working drive will be used to rebuild the mirror on the new disk. This ability to quickly restore data after a failure is a key benefit of RAID 1.

In addition to fault tolerance, RAID 1 also provides a performance benefit in terms of read speeds. Since data is mirrored across multiple drives, the system can access data from either drive, allowing for parallel reading. This means that read operations can be performed faster compared to a single drive, particularly in situations where multiple read requests are being made simultaneously. For applications that involve frequent data retrieval, such as content management systems or media libraries, RAID 1's read performance can significantly improve responsiveness. However, it is important to note that while RAID 1 provides improved read speeds, it does not offer the same level of performance improvement in write operations. Since data must be written to both drives simultaneously, write speeds can be limited by the speed of the individual drives and the RAID controller.

Despite its many advantages, RAID 1 does have some limitations, particularly in terms of storage efficiency. Since the data is duplicated across two or more drives, the total usable storage capacity is effectively halved. For example, if two 1TB drives are used in a RAID 1 array, the total usable storage capacity will be 1TB, as the data is mirrored between the two drives. This can be a disadvantage for users who require large amounts of storage but want to maintain a high level of redundancy. However, for many users, particularly those with smaller storage needs, the redundancy offered by RAID 1 is a worthwhile trade-off for the reduced storage capacity.

Another limitation of RAID 1 is its inability to protect against other forms of data loss, such as accidental deletion, file corruption, or malicious attacks. While RAID 1 ensures that data remains accessible in the event of a drive failure, it does not guard against the possibility of data being inadvertently overwritten or destroyed. For this reason, RAID 1 should be used in conjunction with regular backup strategies to provide comprehensive protection against data loss. Users should ensure that they have a robust backup system in place, ideally with offsite or cloud-based backups, to ensure that their data is fully protected from all potential threats.

RAID 1 is also limited by its scalability. While it is effective for small to medium-sized storage needs, it may not be the best solution for environments that require large-scale data storage. As storage requirements grow, users may find that the need for additional storage capacity or performance improvements necessitates moving to other RAID levels, such as RAID 5 or RAID 10, which offer a better balance between redundancy, performance, and capacity.

Despite these limitations, RAID 1 remains one of the most popular choices for users who prioritize data protection and uptime over performance or storage capacity. Its straightforward design, combined with its ability to protect against drive failures, makes it an ideal solution for a wide range of applications. Whether used in personal computers, small business servers, or enterprise-level systems, RAID 1 ensures that data remains available and secure, even in the event of hardware failure. The simplicity, reliability, and ease of maintenance of RAID 1 make it a valuable tool for anyone seeking to protect their data without the complexities associated with more advanced RAID configurations. For those who need a high level of data protection and can manage the trade-off in storage efficiency, RAID 1 remains one of the best solutions available.

RAID 5: Combining Performance and Redundancy

RAID 5 is one of the most widely used and versatile configurations in the world of data storage. It offers a unique combination of performance, redundancy, and storage efficiency, making it an attractive choice for both enterprise and personal storage systems. RAID 5 achieves this balance by using a method known as striping with parity, which allows data to be spread across multiple drives while still providing fault tolerance in the event of a disk failure. The configuration requires a minimum of three drives, and it delivers significant performance benefits without sacrificing data protection. This makes RAID 5 ideal for environments where both speed and reliability are critical, such as file servers, database systems, and virtualized infrastructures.

The key to RAID 5's design lies in its use of parity, which is a form of error-correction data. In a RAID 5 array, data is striped across multiple drives, similar to RAID 0, but with the addition of parity information. The parity data is not stored on a single drive but is distributed across all the drives in the array. This distribution of parity ensures that even if one drive fails, the missing data can be reconstructed using the parity information stored on the remaining drives. Parity is essentially a mathematical calculation that allows the system to rebuild lost data in the event of a failure. As a result, RAID 5 offers a higher level of data protection compared to RAID 0, which has no redundancy, and it does so without sacrificing too much in terms of storage capacity.

One of the primary advantages of RAID 5 is its ability to balance performance and redundancy. By striping data across multiple drives, RAID 5 improves read and write speeds compared to single-disk storage systems. Data can be read from multiple drives simultaneously, which reduces bottlenecks and speeds up data access. In terms of write operations, RAID 5 also benefits from striping, but the addition of parity means that each write operation involves an extra step of calculating and writing parity data. This can slow down write speeds slightly compared to RAID 0, but the impact on performance is generally minimal, especially when compared to the added benefit of redundancy.

The fault tolerance provided by RAID 5 is another significant advantage. In the event of a single drive failure, the system remains operational, and data can still be accessed without any loss. The missing data is reconstructed using the parity information stored across the remaining drives. While RAID 5 can survive a single drive failure, it is important to note that the system becomes vulnerable to data loss if a second drive fails before the failed drive is replaced and the array is rebuilt. This is why it is essential to monitor the health of drives in a RAID 5 array and replace any failed drives as soon as possible to maintain the integrity of the array.

RAID 5 provides a significant improvement in storage efficiency compared to other RAID configurations that require data duplication. For example, in RAID 1, where data is mirrored across two drives, the total usable storage capacity is halved. In RAID 5, only one drive's worth of capacity is used for parity, regardless of how many drives are in the array. This makes RAID 5 a more efficient use of storage space while still offering protection against data loss. As the number of drives in the RAID 5 array increases, the efficiency of storage increases as well. For instance, in a four-drive RAID 5 array, only one-fourth of the total storage capacity is used for parity, which means the remaining three-fourths can be used for data storage. This storage efficiency makes RAID 5 a popular choice for businesses and individuals who need both high-capacity storage and redundancy.

Despite its many advantages, RAID 5 does have some limitations. One of the primary drawbacks of RAID 5 is its impact on write performance. Because each write operation requires the calculation and writing of parity data, write speeds in RAID 5 can be slower compared to RAID 0 or RAID 1. This is especially noticeable in environments where the system is constantly writing data to the array, such as in database systems or applications that generate large amounts of transactional data. The overhead of parity calculations can also impact overall system performance, particularly if the RAID controller does not have hardware support for parity processing.

Another potential issue with RAID 5 is the time it takes to rebuild an array after a drive failure. When a drive fails in a RAID 5 array, the system enters a degraded mode, where the data is still accessible, but performance is reduced. The system then begins the process of rebuilding the array by using the parity data from the remaining drives to recreate the lost data. This rebuild process can take several hours or even days, depending on the size of the drives and the amount of data stored in the array. During this time, the array is vulnerable to a second drive failure, which could result in data loss. To mitigate this risk, many organizations use hot spares, which are spare drives that are automatically incorporated into the array during the rebuild process, allowing the array to return to full redundancy more quickly.

RAID 5 is also more complex to manage than simpler configurations like RAID 0 or RAID 1. The need to calculate and write parity data adds an extra layer of complexity to the RAID controller and the underlying storage system. Additionally, RAID 5 requires careful monitoring to ensure that drives are functioning correctly and that any failures are quickly addressed. The risk of data loss increases if a drive failure is not detected and replaced in a timely manner. As a result, RAID 5 is best suited for users who have the technical expertise to manage and maintain the array properly.

Despite these challenges, RAID 5 remains one of the most popular RAID configurations for both home and enterprise storage systems. It provides an excellent balance of performance, redundancy, and storage efficiency, making it ideal for applications that require high availability and reliability, such as file servers, web hosting, and database management. The ability to provide fault tolerance with minimal loss of storage capacity makes RAID 5 particularly appealing in environments where data protection is crucial, but where the cost of storage needs to be kept reasonable.

In summary, RAID 5 is a powerful and flexible RAID level that combines the performance benefits of striping with the data protection provided by parity. It strikes an effective balance between speed, reliability, and storage efficiency, making it an excellent choice for a wide range of applications. While it has some limitations, particularly in terms of write performance and rebuild time, the advantages of RAID 5 make it one of the most widely used RAID configurations in modern storage systems. Whether for personal use or enterprise environments, RAID 5 provides an efficient and reliable solution for users who need both performance and redundancy.

RAID 6: Enhanced Redundancy for High Availability

RAID 6 is a configuration that takes redundancy and fault tolerance to the next level, providing enhanced protection for data in environments where high availability is crucial. It is an extension of RAID 5, introducing an additional layer of fault tolerance through the use of double parity. While RAID 5 offers protection against the failure of a single drive, RAID 6 can withstand the simultaneous failure of two drives within the array without losing data. This added redundancy makes RAID 6 an ideal choice for mission-critical applications and large-scale storage systems where uptime is paramount, and data integrity is of the utmost importance.

In RAID 6, data is striped across multiple drives, similar to RAID 5, but with the key difference that two sets of parity information are distributed across the array instead of one. Parity is calculated and stored for each block of data, but in RAID 6, the parity is spread across all the drives in the array, allowing the system to recover data even if two drives fail at the same time. This dual-parity mechanism ensures that RAID 6 provides a higher level of fault tolerance compared to other RAID configurations. The parity data allows the system to reconstruct the lost data from the failed drives, ensuring that the storage system continues to operate without downtime.

RAID 6 offers significant advantages in terms of data protection. Its ability to withstand the failure of two drives provides peace of mind in environments where data loss is unacceptable, such as in large enterprises, data centers, or cloud storage systems. The dual parity ensures that even in the event of multiple failures, the data remains safe and accessible. This level of protection is particularly important in high-availability environments where even brief periods of downtime can result in financial losses, lost productivity, or reputational damage. RAID 6 mitigates the risk of such losses by ensuring that the system remains operational, even when two drives fail simultaneously.

The enhanced redundancy provided by RAID 6 also offers greater peace of mind for organizations that rely on continuous access to their data. For example, in financial institutions or healthcare organizations, where data must be readily available at all times, the ability to survive multiple drive failures without data loss is crucial. RAID 6 is also used extensively in cloud storage systems, where massive amounts of data are stored and accessed by millions of users. In these scenarios, the high availability and fault tolerance of RAID 6 ensure that users experience minimal disruptions to service, even if a failure occurs.

In terms of performance, RAID 6 offers a balance between speed and redundancy. Like RAID 5, RAID 6 stripes data across multiple drives, which improves read performance by allowing data to be accessed from several drives simultaneously. However, the addition of dual parity means that write performance in RAID 6 is generally slower than in RAID 5. This is because, in addition to writing the data itself, the system must also calculate and write two sets of parity data for each write operation. This additional overhead can result in slower write speeds compared to RAID 5, but the trade-off is the enhanced fault tolerance and the ability to recover from the failure of two drives.

The increased redundancy and protection come at the cost of storage efficiency. RAID 6 requires more storage space for the parity data, which reduces the usable capacity of the array. For example, in a four-drive RAID 6 array, the capacity of two drives is used for parity, leaving only the remaining drives available for data storage. This means that RAID 6 offers less usable storage capacity than RAID 5, which only uses the equivalent of one drive for parity. However, the additional protection provided by RAID 6 may justify the trade-off in environments where data security and availability are more important than maximizing storage space.

Despite its advantages, RAID 6 does have some limitations. One of the primary drawbacks is the complexity of rebuilding the array after a drive failure. When a drive fails in a RAID 6 array, the system can continue to function normally, but the data is no longer fully redundant. The array enters a degraded state, and the failed drive must be replaced as soon as possible to restore full redundancy. Rebuilding the array after a failed drive involves reconstructing the lost data using the parity information stored across the remaining drives. This process can be time-consuming, especially in large arrays, and it can place a significant load on the remaining drives. During this rebuild process, the system may experience reduced performance, and if a second drive fails before the rebuild is complete, data loss may occur. For this reason, it is essential to monitor the health of the drives in a RAID 6 array and replace failed drives as quickly as possible.

Another consideration when using RAID 6 is the impact on write performance. The overhead of calculating and writing two sets of parity data means that RAID 6 is not as fast as RAID 0 or RAID 1 for write-intensive applications. While the read performance in RAID 6 is generally good, as data can be accessed from multiple drives in parallel, write operations are slower due to the additional parity calculations. This performance degradation can be mitigated to some extent with the use of advanced RAID controllers that provide hardware-based parity calculation, but the fact remains that RAID 6 is not the best choice for applications that require high-speed write operations, such as real-time data processing or transactional databases.

Despite these challenges, RAID 6 remains an excellent choice for environments that prioritize high availability and data protection over raw performance. The ability to survive the failure of two drives simultaneously makes RAID 6 an attractive option for organizations that cannot afford to experience any downtime or data loss. RAID 6 is commonly used in high-capacity storage arrays, such as those found in enterprise environments, cloud services, and data centers, where data security and continuous availability are essential. It is also used in applications where the risk of data loss must be minimized, such as in backup systems, video surveillance, and disaster recovery systems.

RAID 6 is often used in conjunction with other technologies to further enhance data protection. For example, combining RAID 6 with hot spares—extra drives that can automatically replace a failed drive in the array—can help to speed up the rebuild process and ensure that the system remains fully redundant during a drive failure. Additionally, RAID 6 can be paired with offsite or cloud backups to provide an extra layer of protection against data loss due to catastrophic events, such as natural disasters or cyberattacks.

RAID 6's ability to provide enhanced redundancy for high availability makes it one of the most reliable and resilient RAID configurations available. It offers a unique combination of fault tolerance and storage efficiency, making it a powerful solution for environments where data integrity and system uptime are non-negotiable. Whether in large-scale data centers or critical business applications, RAID 6 ensures that data is protected and always available, even in the face of multiple drive failures. The ability to withstand two simultaneous drive failures without data loss gives organizations the confidence to continue operating smoothly, knowing that their data is safe and accessible.

RAID 10: The Best of Both Worlds

RAID 10, often referred to as RAID 1+0, is a hybrid storage configuration that combines the benefits of two of the most popular RAID levels: RAID 1 and RAID 0. It is designed to offer both the redundancy of RAID 1 (mirroring) and the performance benefits of RAID 0 (striping), creating a solution that delivers the best of both worlds. By combining these two RAID techniques, RAID 10 provides a compelling option for those who need both high performance and high availability in their storage systems. With RAID 10, users can enjoy improved read and write speeds while ensuring that their data is protected from hardware failures, making it an ideal choice for mission-critical applications.

RAID 10 is built by creating pairs of mirrored drives (RAID 1) and then striping data across these mirrored pairs (RAID 0). To implement RAID 10, at least four drives are required. The data is first mirrored on each pair of drives, ensuring that an exact copy of the data exists on two separate drives. Then, the data is striped across the mirrored pairs, which improves performance by allowing data to be read and written simultaneously from multiple disks. This combination of mirroring and striping gives RAID 10 the ability to offer redundancy while maintaining high throughput.

The redundancy in RAID 10 comes from the mirroring aspect, which means that each drive in a mirrored pair holds an identical copy of the data. If one drive in the pair fails, the other drive contains a complete copy of the data, allowing the system to continue operating without data loss. The striped portion of RAID 10, however, enhances performance. Because the data is spread across multiple drives, read and write operations can be performed concurrently, which reduces bottlenecks and increases throughput. This makes RAID 10 a powerful solution for applications that require both data security and fast access times, such as database management systems, video editing, and high-performance computing environments.

One of the key advantages of RAID 10 is its balanced approach to both performance and redundancy. Unlike RAID 5 or RAID 6, which use parity for data protection, RAID 10 provides redundancy through mirroring, which is a simpler and more efficient method. The lack of parity calculations means that RAID 10 can offer superior write performance compared to RAID 5 or RAID 6. This makes RAID 10 an attractive option for environments where high-speed write operations are essential, such as in transactional databases or systems that handle large amounts of small, random write operations.

The performance of RAID 10 is also exceptional when it comes to read speeds. Since data is striped across multiple drives, read operations can be performed in parallel, allowing the system to access data from different drives at the same time. This leads to faster read times, especially in scenarios that involve frequent access to large datasets. RAID 10 is particularly beneficial for workloads that require fast data retrieval, such as in content management systems, web servers, and file servers. The ability to increase read throughput without sacrificing data protection makes RAID 10 a powerful and flexible solution for high-demand environments.

Another significant advantage of RAID 10 is its fault tolerance. Because data is mirrored across pairs of drives, RAID 10 can survive the failure of one drive in each mirrored pair without any loss of data. This gives it a higher level of protection than RAID 0, which offers no redundancy, and even RAID 5, which can only tolerate the failure of a single drive. However, RAID 10 does require at least four drives, which means that the usable storage capacity is only half of the total number of drives in the array. For example, in a four-drive RAID 10 array, the total storage capacity is equivalent to the capacity of two drives, as the other two drives are used for mirroring. While this results in less efficient use of storage space compared to other RAID levels, the trade-off is a high level of redundancy and performance.

RAID 10 is often favored in environments where uptime is critical and where data loss cannot be tolerated. In industries such as healthcare, finance, and e-commerce, where access to data must be continuous and reliable, RAID 10 provides the ideal solution. The ability to survive multiple drive failures without data loss, combined with its high-speed read and write capabilities, makes RAID 10 a perfect fit for businesses that require both performance and data protection. RAID 10 is also well-suited for virtualized environments, where the demands for fast storage access are high and where data availability is essential.

However, there are some considerations to keep in mind when implementing RAID 10. One of the main drawbacks is the cost. Since RAID 10 requires at least four drives, it can be more expensive than other RAID configurations, such as RAID 1 or RAID 5. Additionally, because RAID 10 requires a drive for each mirrored pair, the total storage capacity is limited by the number of drives used in the array. This means that while RAID 10 offers superior performance and redundancy, it is not the most storage-efficient RAID level. For organizations that need to maximize storage capacity while still maintaining redundancy, RAID 5 or RAID 6 may be more suitable options.

RAID 10 also requires careful monitoring and management. While it provides excellent fault tolerance, the failure of more than one drive in a mirrored pair will result in data loss. Therefore, it is essential to replace failed drives promptly and ensure that the array is rebuilt as quickly as possible to maintain redundancy. Additionally, since RAID 10 uses striping, it can be vulnerable to data corruption if a drive fails during a write operation. To mitigate this risk, users should implement regular backup procedures in addition to using RAID 10 for data protection.

In terms of scalability, RAID 10 has its limitations. While it can be expanded by adding more drives to the array, the need for mirroring means that additional drives must be added in pairs, which can limit the flexibility of the system. For larger storage environments that require more efficient scalability, other RAID levels, such as RAID 5 or RAID 6, may be more suitable.

Despite these considerations, RAID 10 remains one of the most reliable and high-performance RAID configurations available. Its combination of striping for speed and mirroring for redundancy makes it a versatile and powerful solution for environments where both data security and high throughput are required. The trade-offs in terms of storage efficiency and cost are often outweighed by the benefits of enhanced performance and fault tolerance, making RAID 10 a popular choice for businesses and individuals who need the best of both worlds in their storage systems. Whether for database management, high-performance computing, or virtualized environments, RAID 10 offers a robust solution that ensures data is both safe and accessible, even in the face of hardware failures.

RAID 50: A Hybrid of RAID 5 and RAID 0

RAID 50 is a hybrid configuration that combines the features of RAID 5 and RAID 0 to deliver a balanced solution for users who require both high performance and data redundancy. This RAID level, sometimes referred to as RAID 5+0, offers the fault tolerance of RAID 5 along with the improved speed of RAID 0, making it an attractive choice for environments where both data protection and performance are critical. RAID 50 achieves this by striping data across multiple RAID 5 arrays, resulting in a configuration that provides both fault tolerance through parity and the performance benefits of data striping.

In RAID 50, multiple RAID 5 arrays are created and then striped together. This means that data is first distributed across multiple drives within each RAID 5 array, with parity information spread across those drives. The result is that each RAID 5 array can protect against the failure of one drive, as the parity data allows for the reconstruction of lost data if a drive fails. Then, the data from these individual RAID 5 arrays is striped across additional drives, similar to how RAID 0 works. This striping of data enhances the system's performance by allowing read and write operations to be distributed across multiple drives, reducing bottlenecks and improving throughput.

The key advantage of RAID 50 is its ability to combine the best features of RAID 5 and RAID 0. By using RAID 5 for redundancy, RAID 50 ensures that the data remains protected in the event of a drive failure. The parity information stored in each RAID 5 array enables the system to reconstruct lost data and continue functioning normally, even when one drive fails within a RAID 5 set. This makes RAID 50 a highly resilient storage solution for environments where uptime and data integrity are essential. Additionally, the striping inherent in RAID 0 provides a significant boost to performance, particularly in read-intensive applications. With RAID 50, data can be read from multiple RAID 5 arrays simultaneously, resulting in faster data access times and increased throughput.

RAID 50 is particularly useful for high-performance environments, such as database servers, web hosting, and large-scale data storage systems. These types of applications often require a storage solution that can handle large amounts of data with minimal latency. RAID 50 addresses this need by combining the fault tolerance and storage efficiency of RAID 5 with the increased performance of RAID 0. The striping of data across multiple RAID 5 arrays ensures that the system can handle multiple read and write requests concurrently, resulting in faster data processing and improved system responsiveness. This makes RAID 50 ideal for environments where both speed and reliability are critical for maintaining optimal performance.

While RAID 50 offers substantial benefits, there are also some limitations to consider. One of the primary drawbacks of RAID 50 is that it requires a minimum of six drives, which makes it more expensive to implement compared to simpler configurations like RAID 1 or RAID 5. In a RAID 50 array, multiple RAID 5 sets must be created, and each RAID 5 set must have at least three drives. The cost of acquiring additional drives can be a barrier for smaller businesses or individuals who are looking for a more budget-friendly solution. However, for larger enterprises that require high performance and redundancy, the added cost is often justified by the increased data protection and faster speeds.

Another potential issue with RAID 50 is the complexity of managing and maintaining the array. RAID 50 combines two different RAID levels, which can make it more difficult to configure and troubleshoot compared to other RAID configurations. Managing multiple RAID 5 sets within a RAID 50 array requires a higher level of expertise and can involve more complex processes for monitoring drive health, handling failures, and performing rebuilds. Additionally, because RAID 50 relies on the parity data in RAID 5 for fault tolerance, the rebuild process can be time-consuming, particularly when dealing with large amounts of data. If a drive fails in one of the RAID 5 sets, the system must rebuild the lost data using the parity information, which can place significant load on the remaining drives and impact overall system performance during the rebuild process.

RAID 50 also suffers from the same performance issues associated with RAID 5 when it comes to write operations. While the striping in RAID 0 improves read performance, write operations in RAID 50 can still be slower than in RAID 0 or RAID 1 due to the overhead of calculating and writing parity data. Each write operation must update both the data and the parity information, which can introduce delays, especially in write-intensive applications. However, the performance trade-off is generally acceptable for most use cases, particularly when the benefits of redundancy and overall system performance are considered.

Despite these limitations, RAID 50 is an excellent solution for users who need a balance between performance and redundancy. It provides the data protection of RAID 5 while delivering the high throughput of RAID 0, making it well-suited for demanding applications such as file servers, email systems, and large-scale storage arrays. The redundancy offered by RAID 5 ensures that data is protected against drive failures, while the striping across multiple arrays enhances performance, making it an ideal choice for systems that require both speed and reliability.

RAID 50 can also be beneficial in environments where scalability is important. As the storage needs of a system grow, RAID 50 allows additional drives to be added to the array without significant reconfiguration. This flexibility makes it possible to scale the storage capacity while maintaining high performance and redundancy. In addition, RAID 50 can be used in conjunction with other technologies, such as SSDs or hot spares, to further enhance performance and reliability. SSDs, in particular, can be used to speed up read and write operations, making RAID 50 even more suitable for high-performance applications.

One of the most significant benefits of RAID 50 is its ability to provide fault tolerance while maintaining a high level of storage efficiency. Unlike RAID 1, which duplicates data across multiple drives, RAID 50 only requires the equivalent of one drive's worth of space for parity across each RAID 5 set. This allows RAID 50 to offer better storage utilization compared to mirroring configurations, such as RAID 1, while still providing protection against data loss. The combination of performance, redundancy, and storage efficiency makes RAID 50 a versatile and powerful solution for many different types of data storage needs.

RAID 50 offers an excellent solution for users who need both performance and fault tolerance, providing a balanced approach that ensures both fast access to data and protection against drive failures. It is particularly valuable in enterprise environments where high availability and speed are paramount. Although it requires more drives and may involve greater complexity in configuration and maintenance, RAID 50's ability to combine the strengths of RAID 5 and RAID 0 makes it an attractive choice for users who require both high performance and redundancy in their storage systems.

RAID 60: The Hybrid Approach to RAID 6 and RAID 0

RAID 60, a hybrid configuration that combines the best features of RAID 6 and RAID 0, is designed to provide both enhanced data protection and performance. This setup offers a significant improvement over other RAID levels by utilizing dual parity from RAID 6 and the striping from RAID 0. The result is a storage solution that not only ensures high availability through fault tolerance but also boosts performance for high-demand environments. RAID 60 is particularly well-suited for large-scale storage systems where data protection and system speed are both critical.

At the heart of RAID 60's design is its combination of RAID 6's double parity and RAID 0's striping. RAID 6 provides fault tolerance by storing two sets of parity information across the drives in the array, allowing the system to continue functioning even if two drives fail simultaneously. RAID 0, on the other hand, uses striping to spread data across multiple drives, allowing for faster read and write operations by enabling simultaneous access to different parts of the data. RAID 60 takes these two concepts and integrates them, ensuring that data is not only protected by dual parity but is also accessed quickly due to the striping feature.

In a RAID 60 array, multiple RAID 6 arrays are created, and then these arrays are striped together. This means that the data is first distributed across multiple drives within each RAID 6 array, with two parity blocks providing fault tolerance. Then, these RAID 6 sets are striped across additional drives, similar to the striping technique used in RAID 0. This striping process enhances the performance of the system, as it allows for parallel data access across multiple arrays. The combination of RAID 6's redundancy and RAID 0's speed results in a solution that can handle both large amounts of data and high transaction rates without sacrificing performance.

One of the major advantages of RAID 60 is its ability to handle large amounts of data while ensuring redundancy. The dual parity in RAID 6 means that the system can tolerate two drive failures in each RAID 6 array, a feature that makes RAID 60 particularly appealing for environments that require high levels of data availability and reliability. For example, large-scale data centers, enterprise storage solutions, and cloud computing platforms benefit from RAID 60's ability to prevent data loss even when two drives in one of the RAID 6 arrays fail. This level of fault tolerance is essential in situations where even brief periods of downtime can result in significant losses or disruptions.

Performance is another area where RAID 60 excels. The striping across multiple RAID 6 arrays allows for faster data access and improved throughput. Data can be read and written to several drives in parallel, significantly increasing system speed. RAID 60 is particularly beneficial in applications where high-speed access to large datasets is required, such as in video editing, data analytics, or virtualization. For these applications, the ability to access data quickly is paramount, and RAID 60 offers an excellent balance of both performance and redundancy to meet these demands.

Despite its performance and redundancy benefits, RAID 60 is not without its limitations. One of the primary drawbacks of RAID 60 is its storage efficiency. Since RAID 6 uses two sets of parity, the usable capacity of the array is reduced by the equivalent of two drives for every RAID 6 set. For example, in a six-drive RAID 60 array, the total storage capacity is equivalent to four drives, as two drives are used for parity. This reduced storage efficiency can be a concern for environments that require large amounts of storage, as the overhead of dual parity reduces the available capacity for data storage. However, the trade-off between storage efficiency and redundancy is often acceptable for users who prioritize data protection and performance over raw storage capacity.

RAID 60 also requires more drives than other RAID configurations to provide the same level of redundancy. At a minimum, RAID 60 requires eight drives, as it consists of at least two RAID 6 sets, each requiring a minimum of four drives. This can result in higher upfront costs for purchasing the necessary drives and can be a consideration for users with limited budgets. However, for businesses or organizations that require both high availability and high performance, the benefits of RAID 60 often outweigh the initial investment.

Another consideration when using RAID 60 is the complexity of the system. Since RAID 60 is essentially a combination of two different RAID levels, it can be more challenging to configure and manage than simpler RAID configurations like RAID 1 or RAID 5. Monitoring the health of the drives, performing rebuilds after a failure, and ensuring that the system remains balanced can require more effort and technical expertise. Furthermore, as with all RAID systems, it is important to replace failed drives as soon as possible to maintain redundancy and prevent data loss.

The rebuild process in RAID 60 can also be time-consuming, especially in larger arrays with more data. When a drive fails in one of the RAID 6 sets, the array enters a degraded mode, and the system must rebuild the lost data using the parity information from the remaining drives. This rebuild process can be slow and resource-intensive, particularly if the array contains large amounts of data. During the rebuild, the remaining drives are under heavy load, which can impact system performance. Additionally, the system is vulnerable to further drive failures during the rebuild process, so it is critical to monitor the health of the drives and replace any failed components as quickly as possible.

RAID 60's ability to combine the redundancy of RAID 6 with the performance benefits of RAID 0 makes it an excellent solution for enterprise environments where both data security and speed are essential. In applications that require high throughput and low latency, such as in financial institutions, scientific research, or cloud services, RAID 60 offers a reliable and efficient storage solution. By providing the ability to withstand multiple drive failures while delivering high-speed data access, RAID 60 ensures that organizations can continue operating without interruption, even in the face of hardware issues.

Additionally, RAID 60 can be used in conjunction with other technologies to further enhance its performance and reliability. For instance, solid-state drives (SSDs) can be incorporated into a RAID 60 array to increase read and write speeds, particularly in applications that require extremely fast data access. Hot spares, which are extra drives that automatically replace failed drives in the array, can also be used to speed up the rebuild process and maintain redundancy during a failure.

RAID 60 is a versatile and powerful storage configuration that combines the best aspects of RAID 6 and RAID 0. By offering both redundancy and performance, it provides a balanced solution for users who require high levels of data protection and fast access to large datasets. While it comes with some limitations in terms of storage efficiency and complexity, RAID 60 remains a valuable choice for organizations and enterprises that require a reliable and high-performance storage solution. Its ability to handle large-scale data while ensuring high availability and fault tolerance makes it a popular choice for critical applications in industries where data loss or downtime is not an option.

RAID 2 and RAID 3: Rare Configurations

RAID 2 and RAID 3 are both relatively rare configurations in the world of data storage systems, largely overshadowed by other more popular RAID levels like RAID 0, RAID 1, RAID 5, and RAID 6. While they offer unique benefits in terms of data protection and performance, they have been largely replaced or supplanted by other RAID levels that offer similar advantages with greater efficiency and ease of implementation. However, understanding the principles behind these RAID configurations can provide valuable insight into the evolution of RAID technology and the underlying concepts of redundancy, speed, and fault tolerance.

RAID 2, one of the more unusual configurations, is based on the concept of bit-level striping. In RAID 2, data is split into bits, and each bit is written to a separate disk in the array. This means that each disk in the array stores a single bit of data, and data is read or written by accessing the appropriate bit from each disk in parallel. RAID 2 utilizes a Hamming code for error correction, which allows the system to detect and correct errors in data during the read and write processes. A dedicated disk is used for storing the error correction codes, ensuring that the system can correct any single-bit errors that may occur during data transmission or storage.

The primary advantage of RAID 2 is its ability to provide a very high level of error correction, making it one of the most reliable RAID configurations in terms of data integrity. Since it uses bit-level striping and includes error correction codes, RAID 2 can detect and correct errors in real-time, ensuring that data remains accurate and intact. This makes it an appealing choice for environments where data integrity is absolutely critical, such as in scientific computing, aerospace, or other specialized fields where even the smallest error in data could have significant consequences.

However, the complexity of RAID 2 also makes it less practical for general use. The bit-level striping requires a large number of disks for relatively small amounts of data, which makes the system inefficient in terms of both storage capacity and cost. For instance, in a RAID 2 array with 8 data disks, a separate disk is required for each bit of data, resulting in 8 disks just for the storage of a small amount of information. This makes RAID 2 extremely inefficient in terms of disk usage, and the overhead required for the error correction codes further reduces the usable capacity of the array. Additionally, the need for parallel access to all the disks in the array during every read or write operation places significant demands on the system, which can lead to slower performance compared to other RAID configurations.

Because of these inefficiencies and its reliance on bit-level striping, RAID 2 has been largely replaced by other, more efficient RAID levels. For example, RAID 5 and RAID 6 provide similar levels of data protection using block-level striping and parity, while requiring fewer disks and offering better overall performance. As a result, RAID 2 has become obsolete in modern storage systems, with few, if any, applications still using it in production environments. Despite its historical significance as one of the first RAID configurations, its practical applications are extremely limited.

RAID 3, on the other hand, is a more practical RAID configuration, though it is still relatively rare compared to other RAID levels. RAID 3 uses byte-level striping, where data is divided into bytes instead of bits, and it stores this data across multiple disks in parallel. One key feature of RAID 3 is its use of a dedicated parity disk, which stores the parity data for the entire array. Parity is a form of error correction that allows the system to rebuild lost data if a drive fails. By using a single parity disk, RAID 3 can provide fault tolerance for the array while still maintaining relatively high performance.

The use of byte-level striping in RAID 3 means that data can be read and written more efficiently than in RAID 2, as the system only needs to access whole bytes instead of individual bits. This results in better performance, especially when reading large blocks of data. The dedicated parity disk in RAID 3 allows for the recovery of data in the event of a single drive failure, providing fault tolerance similar to RAID 5. If one drive in the array fails, the system can reconstruct the lost data using the parity information stored on the dedicated disk. This makes RAID 3 a reliable choice for environments where data availability is critical and where performance is still a concern.

However, RAID 3 also has its limitations. One of the primary drawbacks is the use of a single parity disk, which can become a bottleneck for write operations. Since all write operations must update the parity disk, this creates a situation where the parity disk is constantly being accessed, leading to potential performance degradation. For systems with heavy write operations, RAID 3 may not provide the same level of performance as other RAID configurations like RAID 5 or RAID 10, which distribute the parity data across multiple disks. Additionally, RAID 3 can suffer from underutilization of the available disks when dealing with random access patterns, as the system is optimized for sequential data access.

Another issue with RAID 3 is its complexity. The requirement for a dedicated parity disk means that RAID 3 can be more difficult to configure and manage than simpler RAID levels like RAID 1 or RAID 0. The overhead involved in managing the parity disk and ensuring that it is properly synchronized with the other disks in the array can make RAID 3 more challenging to maintain. Additionally, RAID 3 requires a minimum of three disks to function, which is more than the two-disk minimum required for RAID 1 or RAID 0. The additional cost of the parity disk and the potential performance limitations make RAID 3 less attractive compared to other RAID levels that offer better performance and more efficient data protection.

While RAID 2 and RAID 3 both offer unique advantages in terms of data protection and fault tolerance, their practical applications are limited by their inefficiencies and the availability of better alternatives. RAID 2, with its bit-level striping and Hamming code error correction, provides an incredibly high level of data integrity, but it is inefficient in terms of storage capacity and performance. RAID 3, while more practical and providing better performance than RAID 2, suffers from bottlenecks due to its dedicated parity disk and is better suited for sequential access workloads rather than environments with heavy random access demands.

Both RAID 2 and RAID 3 are largely obsolete in modern storage systems, having been replaced by other, more efficient RAID levels like RAID 5 and RAID 6, which offer similar levels of fault tolerance and performance with greater storage efficiency. Nonetheless, these configurations remain important from a historical perspective, illustrating the early development of RAID technology and the ongoing quest to balance performance, redundancy, and efficiency in data storage systems.

RAID 4: A Redundant Alternative to RAID 5

RAID 4 is a less commonly used RAID configuration that provides redundancy through the use of parity, making it an alternative to RAID 5 for users who need data protection and fault tolerance without resorting to full mirroring. Like RAID 5, RAID 4 utilizes parity data to protect against the failure of one drive, but it employs a slightly different approach by storing all the parity information on a single dedicated disk. This unique design has both advantages and limitations that make RAID 4 suitable for certain use cases, though it has largely been overshadowed by RAID 5, which offers similar fault tolerance but with better performance and storage efficiency.

At its core, RAID 4 is built upon the concept of block-level striping, where data is split into chunks and distributed across multiple drives. However, unlike RAID 5, where parity is distributed across all the drives in the array, RAID 4 stores the parity data on a dedicated disk. The parity is calculated based on the data that is written to the array and serves as a form of error correction. In the event that a drive fails, the missing data can be reconstructed by using the parity information stored on the dedicated parity disk. This allows the system to continue operating even when one of the drives fails, providing a level of redundancy similar to RAID 5.

One of the key advantages of RAID 4 is its ability to provide fault tolerance while using less storage space than RAID 1, which requires mirroring the data across multiple drives. By using parity, RAID 4 only requires the equivalent of one drive's capacity for redundancy, regardless of the number of drives in the array. This makes RAID 4 a more storage-efficient solution than RAID 1, especially in larger arrays. The ability to store data across multiple disks while maintaining fault tolerance makes RAID 4 an attractive option for users who need to maximize the use of available storage space without sacrificing data protection.

In terms of performance, RAID 4 offers improvements over single-drive systems and RAID 1, particularly for read operations. Since data is striped across multiple drives, RAID 4 can access data from multiple disks simultaneously, allowing for faster read speeds. This makes RAID 4 a good option for applications that require high read throughput, such as file servers or web hosting. However, RAID 4's write performance can be a limitation. Because all the parity data is stored on a single disk, every write operation must update the parity disk in addition to writing the data to the other drives. This creates a bottleneck, as the parity disk becomes a point of contention for write operations. The single parity disk can quickly become overloaded, which can significantly degrade write performance, especially in environments with high write activity or frequent data updates.

RAID 4's reliance on a single dedicated parity disk also introduces potential risks. While the system can tolerate the failure of one drive, the failure of the parity disk itself can result in the loss of the entire array. This is a significant drawback, as the redundancy provided by RAID 4 depends entirely on the parity disk being operational. If the parity disk fails, the array becomes vulnerable to data loss, as there would be no parity data available to reconstruct the lost information from a failed drive. In contrast, RAID 5 distributes parity data across all the drives in the array, reducing the risk of a single point of failure and making it more resilient in the event of a disk failure.

Another limitation of RAID 4 is the rebuild process. When a drive fails in a RAID 4 array, the system uses the parity data from the dedicated disk to rebuild the lost data. While this is an effective way to restore data, the process can be slow and resource-intensive, especially in larger arrays. During the rebuild, the system must calculate and write large amounts of data, which places additional load on the remaining drives. This can result in degraded performance during the rebuild process, and if another drive fails during this time, the array may lose data. The rebuild process is also more time-consuming compared to RAID 5, as it involves using parity data from a single disk instead of multiple drives.

RAID 4 is also not as scalable as other RAID configurations. The performance of the array can degrade as more drives are added, as the dedicated parity disk becomes a bottleneck for write operations. In larger arrays, the risk of the parity disk becoming overloaded increases, which can lead to significant performance degradation. RAID 5, in contrast, distributes parity data across all drives, which helps to balance the load and maintain consistent performance as the array grows. This makes RAID 5 a more scalable option for users who need to expand their storage capacity while maintaining good performance.

Despite these limitations, RAID 4 has its place in certain applications where high read performance and fault tolerance are essential, but where write-intensive workloads are not a significant concern. RAID 4 can be suitable for environments where the data is primarily read-heavy, such as in archival storage or data retrieval systems. In these cases, the performance bottleneck associated with the single parity disk may not be as noticeable, and the array can still deliver improved read speeds compared to traditional single-disk storage solutions.

One of the advantages of RAID 4, compared to RAID 5, is its simplicity in terms of understanding and implementation. RAID 4's design is relatively straightforward, as it only requires one additional disk for parity, making it simpler to configure compared to RAID 5, which involves distributing parity data across all drives. This simplicity can make RAID 4 a good option for smaller-scale systems or for users who are new to RAID configurations and want a basic understanding of how data protection and fault tolerance work.

However, RAID 4 is generally not recommended for large-scale enterprise applications, particularly those that require high write performance. For users who need a more efficient and reliable solution, RAID 5 is usually the preferred choice, as it offers the same level of fault tolerance with better performance and scalability. RAID 5's ability to distribute parity data across all drives helps alleviate the bottleneck caused by the single parity disk in RAID 4, making it a more balanced and resilient configuration overall.

In summary, RAID 4 provides a redundancy option that is based on block-level striping with a dedicated parity disk. It offers fault tolerance similar to RAID 5 but suffers from performance bottlenecks due to the reliance on a single parity disk for write operations. The system is most beneficial in environments where read performance is more important than write performance, but it is less scalable and more vulnerable to failure of the parity disk. Although RAID 4 has largely been replaced by RAID 5 in most applications, it remains a historical part of RAID technology and provides insights into the evolution of fault-tolerant storage systems. For users who prioritize data protection and can manage the write bottlenecks, RAID 4 still offers a viable solution for certain types of storage systems.

Nested RAID Levels: Combining Multiple RAID Configurations

Nested RAID levels, or hybrid RAID configurations, represent a combination of two or more standard RAID levels, combining their strengths to provide greater flexibility in terms of performance, fault tolerance, and storage efficiency. These configurations aim to take advantage of the best aspects of multiple RAID levels to meet the demands of complex data storage environments. By combining different RAID techniques, such as striping, mirroring, and parity, nested RAID levels can offer more customized solutions for specific applications, addressing the limitations that individual RAID levels might present on their own. The most common nested RAID levels are RAID 10 (RAID 1+0), RAID 50 (RAID 5+0), and RAID 60 (RAID 6+0), each of which offers a unique balance of performance, redundancy, and capacity.

RAID 10, a combination of RAID 1 (mirroring) and RAID 0 (striping), is one of the most popular nested RAID configurations. In RAID 10, data is mirrored across pairs of drives for redundancy, and then those mirrored pairs are striped together to increase performance. This configuration provides the redundancy of RAID 1, meaning that if one drive in a pair fails, the other drive will still contain a complete copy of the data. At the same time, RAID 10 benefits from the performance enhancement of RAID 0, which allows data to be read and written to multiple drives simultaneously, improving throughput. As a result, RAID 10 offers a combination of both fault tolerance and high performance, making it an ideal choice for environments that require both.

For example, RAID 10 is widely used in applications such as database servers, high-performance computing, and virtualized environments, where both fast data access and high availability are critical. The major benefit of RAID 10 is that it provides excellent read and write performance while ensuring that data remains protected in case of a drive failure. It also has relatively straightforward management compared to other more complex RAID configurations, like RAID 5 or RAID 6. However, the primary disadvantage of RAID 10 is that it requires double the number of drives for a given usable storage capacity, as data is mirrored across pairs of drives. This can result in a higher cost per gigabyte of usable storage compared to other configurations that use parity.

RAID 50, a hybrid of RAID 5 and RAID 0, combines the benefits of RAID 5's fault tolerance with the speed of RAID 0. In a RAID 50 array, multiple RAID 5 arrays are created, and these arrays are then striped together using RAID 0. This configuration allows for both improved performance and fault tolerance, as the striping of data across multiple RAID 5 arrays boosts read and write speeds, while the parity in each RAID 5 set provides protection against the failure of a single drive. RAID 50 is particularly useful for environments that require large amounts of storage and need to balance the trade-off between redundancy and performance.

RAID 50 is often used in scenarios such as large-scale data storage systems, file servers, and applications that require high throughput, such as media production or large database systems. The ability to survive the failure of one drive in each RAID 5 set without losing data is a significant advantage, making RAID 50 a reliable choice for enterprise-level systems. Furthermore, RAID 50's performance improvements over regular RAID 5 come from the striping of data across multiple arrays, which enhances data access speeds. However, like RAID 5, RAID 50 is not immune to the write penalty that comes with parity calculation. Although it performs better than RAID 5 in most cases, write operations can still be slower than in RAID 0 or RAID 10 due to the need to update parity data for every write operation.

RAID 60, a combination of RAID 6 and RAID 0, further enhances the redundancy of RAID 50 by adding an additional layer of protection. In RAID 60, multiple RAID 6 arrays are created, and these arrays are then striped together using RAID 0. RAID 6 offers double parity, meaning it can tolerate the failure of two drives in each RAID 6 set, providing a higher level of fault tolerance than RAID 5 or RAID 50. By combining RAID 6's dual parity with RAID 0's striping, RAID 60 offers the same performance benefits of RAID 0 and the increased redundancy of RAID 6, making it an attractive choice for applications where data protection is of the utmost importance.

RAID 60 is commonly used in environments such as data centers, cloud storage, and high-availability systems, where the reliability and performance of data storage are critical. The double parity provided by RAID 6 allows RAID 60 to survive two drive failures in each RAID 6 set, making it a more fault-tolerant option than RAID 50. However, this redundancy comes at the cost of storage efficiency, as the additional parity disks reduce the total usable capacity of the array. RAID 60 also inherits the write penalty associated with parity-based RAID levels, meaning that while read performance is typically excellent, write operations can still be slower than with non-parity RAID levels like RAID 0 or RAID 10.

The primary benefit of nested RAID levels like RAID 10, RAID 50, and RAID 60 is their ability to balance multiple factors—performance, redundancy, and storage efficiency—depending on the needs of the user. These configurations allow for more customized storage solutions, catering to specific workloads that require a combination of fast data access and high availability. For example, RAID 10 is ideal for environments where both read and write performance are critical, and data protection through mirroring is essential. RAID 50, on the other hand, is better suited for environments that require large storage capacities with a focus on read-intensive workloads, while RAID 60 is a good option for mission-critical applications that require the highest level of fault tolerance, such as disaster recovery and backup systems.

Despite their many advantages, nested RAID levels also come with certain trade-offs. One of the major downsides of RAID 10, RAID 50, and RAID 60 is that they require more disks than single-level RAID configurations. For example, RAID 10 requires at least four disks, RAID 50 requires a minimum of six disks, and RAID 60 requires at least eight disks. This can make these configurations more expensive to implement, especially in environments where storage capacity is a concern. Additionally, while these configurations offer fault tolerance, they do not protect against all forms of data loss. For example, RAID 10 and RAID 50 are vulnerable to data loss if two drives fail simultaneously within the same RAID 1 or RAID 5 set, respectively, while RAID 60's double parity can still be affected if more than two drives fail within a RAID 6 array.

Another challenge of nested RAID configurations is their complexity in terms of setup, maintenance, and management. Configuring and managing RAID 10, RAID 50, and RAID 60 can be more complicated than simpler RAID levels, as they involve multiple RAID arrays and a greater number of disks. This complexity can make troubleshooting more difficult, especially in large-scale environments where monitoring disk health and rebuilding arrays after drive failures is crucial. Furthermore, the rebuild process in these configurations can be time-consuming and resource-intensive, especially when dealing with large amounts of data.

Nested RAID levels provide a powerful solution for users who need to balance performance and redundancy in their storage systems. By combining the strengths of multiple RAID configurations, RAID 10, RAID 50, and RAID 60 offer enhanced capabilities for demanding applications that require both data protection and high throughput. These hybrid solutions continue to be widely used in enterprise environments, data centers, and other industries that require reliable, high-performance storage solutions. However, users must carefully consider the trade-offs in terms of cost, complexity, and storage efficiency when choosing the best RAID configuration for their needs.

Virtual RAID: Storage Virtualization and Its Benefits

Virtual RAID, also known as storage virtualization, represents a modern approach to data storage management that abstracts and consolidates physical storage resources into a single, virtualized storage pool. This approach has gained significant traction in both enterprise and small-scale environments due to its ability to improve storage efficiency, flexibility, and scalability. Unlike traditional RAID configurations, where physical disks are directly tied to the storage array and managed individually, virtual RAID decouples the storage hardware from the underlying operating system and application layer, offering a more dynamic and streamlined method of managing data storage.

At its core, storage virtualization allows administrators to manage storage resources from a centralized point of control without having to be concerned with the specifics of the underlying hardware. This means that virtual storage systems can integrate various types of storage media, including traditional hard drives, solid-state drives, and even network-attached storage (NAS) or storage area networks (SAN). This abstraction layer makes it possible to pool resources from different physical devices, presenting them as a unified storage environment. The flexibility this offers in terms of resource management and the ability to scale storage capacity seamlessly is one of the key benefits of virtual RAID.

One of the primary advantages of virtual RAID is improved storage efficiency. In traditional RAID systems, the allocation of storage is typically fixed, with specific disks assigned to particular RAID levels for redundancy or performance. This fixed nature often leads to inefficient utilization of available storage space, especially in cases where certain disks are underutilized while others are fully populated. Storage virtualization overcomes this by allowing data to be dynamically distributed across all available storage resources, regardless of the specific type of disk or device. This means that virtual RAID systems can adjust the allocation of data based on current needs, improving overall storage efficiency.

Virtual RAID also offers enhanced scalability compared to traditional RAID setups. As the storage needs of an organization grow, virtual RAID allows for the seamless addition of storage resources without significant disruption or reconfiguration. New physical devices, whether local or network-based, can be easily integrated into the virtual storage pool, expanding capacity without requiring the system to be taken offline or undergoing complex setup procedures. This scalability is particularly important for organizations that expect to scale their storage needs over time or those that operate in dynamic environments where data storage requirements fluctuate. The ability to scale resources on-demand without having to manually configure individual RAID arrays streamlines operations and significantly reduces administrative overhead.

Another key benefit of virtual RAID is improved data management and disaster recovery capabilities. Because storage virtualization abstracts the underlying physical devices, it simplifies the management of data across multiple storage systems. In a traditional RAID environment, data management and recovery often require intricate knowledge of the specific configurations and physical layout of the RAID arrays. With virtual RAID, data can be more easily backed up, replicated, and restored, as the system treats the entire storage pool as a single entity rather than managing individual disks. This simplifies processes such as data migration, backups, and disaster recovery, making it easier for organizations to ensure business continuity in the event of hardware failure or other catastrophic events.

Furthermore, virtual RAID systems often include built-in redundancy and fault tolerance mechanisms that are not limited to the physical disks. Many virtualized storage solutions allow for the creation of virtual copies of data that can be replicated to remote locations or to cloud storage services. This provides an added layer of protection and ensures that data is always accessible, even if a local storage system fails. The ability to replicate data across multiple locations reduces the risk of data loss and ensures that critical data remains accessible, regardless of the circumstances.

Virtual RAID also supports more advanced storage management features, such as thin provisioning, which allows for more efficient use of storage resources. Thin provisioning allows administrators to allocate storage space to users or applications without physically committing the entire amount of disk space in advance. Instead, only the storage that is actually in use is allocated, which maximizes storage efficiency and prevents over-provisioning. This is particularly beneficial in environments where storage demand is difficult to predict, as it ensures that resources are allocated only when they are needed, without unnecessary overhead.

In addition to thin provisioning, virtual RAID systems often support automated tiering, which allows for data to be automatically moved between different types of storage media based on access patterns and performance requirements. For example, frequently accessed data might be moved to faster, more expensive storage devices, such as solid-state drives, while infrequently accessed data can be moved to slower, more cost-effective storage devices like hard disk drives. This tiered approach to storage ensures that performance is optimized without requiring manual intervention, and it helps organizations reduce costs by storing data on the most appropriate storage medium based on its importance and usage.

One of the challenges of virtual RAID is the complexity of implementing and managing a virtualized storage environment. While traditional RAID configurations are relatively straightforward, involving direct management of physical disks and arrays, virtual RAID requires more advanced knowledge and expertise. The abstraction layer that enables the pooling and management of various storage devices adds a layer of complexity to system administration, and issues such as virtual machine storage, storage virtualization protocols, and integration with existing infrastructure must be carefully considered. Additionally, the performance of virtual RAID systems can be affected by factors such as network latency and the overall efficiency of the underlying virtualization platform. This makes it essential for organizations to carefully plan their storage infrastructure and ensure that they have the necessary resources to maintain and monitor a virtualized storage environment.

Despite these challenges, virtual RAID offers significant advantages, especially in terms of flexibility, scalability, and data protection. The ability to abstract storage resources and manage them through a centralized interface is particularly valuable in environments where storage demands are constantly changing or growing. For example, businesses that deal with large volumes of unstructured data, such as media files, can benefit from the flexibility that virtual RAID provides in terms of expanding storage capacity and managing multiple storage devices seamlessly. Similarly, organizations that need to ensure high availability and disaster recovery capabilities can take advantage of the replication and fault tolerance features of virtual RAID to protect their critical data.

As data storage requirements continue to grow and the need for more flexible and scalable solutions increases, virtual RAID will continue to play an important role in meeting the demands of modern storage environments. Its ability to combine different types of storage devices into a single, virtualized storage pool provides organizations with a powerful tool for managing their data, ensuring high availability, and improving overall efficiency. While there are some challenges associated with implementing virtual RAID, the benefits it offers make it a valuable solution for businesses and organizations looking to optimize their storage infrastructure and keep pace with the demands of the digital age.

Software vs. Hardware RAID: A Comparison

When configuring a RAID array, one of the most important decisions that users and system administrators face is whether to implement the RAID system through software or hardware. Both software RAID and hardware RAID have their respective advantages and disadvantages, and the choice between the two depends on factors such as cost, performance requirements, scalability, and the specific needs of the organization or individual using the storage system. Understanding the differences between these two approaches can help guide the decision-making process, ensuring that the chosen solution aligns with the intended application.

Software RAID uses the host operating system to manage the RAID configuration. This means that the RAID array is created and managed entirely through software, often with the help of the operating system's built-in RAID tools or third-party software. In this setup, the CPU and system resources are responsible for the RAID calculations, including tasks like data striping, mirroring, and parity calculations. As a result, the operating system plays a significant role in the performance of the RAID system.

One of the primary benefits of software RAID is its low cost. Since no specialized hardware is required, users can create a RAID array with just the existing system resources and drives. This makes software RAID an attractive option for home users or small businesses that need a cost-effective way to implement RAID without investing in additional hardware. Additionally, software RAID is typically more flexible than hardware RAID, as it is not tied to any specific hardware controller and can be used across a wide range of devices and operating systems. For example, software RAID can be easily implemented on any server or personal computer running compatible software, regardless of the brand of hardware or disk drives being used.

Another advantage of software RAID is the ease of setup and configuration. Many modern operating systems, including Windows, Linux, and macOS, provide built-in RAID support, meaning that users can create and manage RAID arrays without needing additional software or hardware. In most cases, users simply need to select the desired RAID level and specify the disks to be used, and the system will handle the rest. This simplicity makes software RAID an appealing choice for those who need a straightforward, no-frills solution for their storage needs.

However, software RAID also has its drawbacks. One of the main disadvantages is that it places a significant burden on the system's CPU and memory. Since the operating system handles all RAID operations, the performance of the RAID array can be affected by the available processing power and system resources. In systems with limited resources or when using RAID levels that require heavy parity calculations, such as RAID 5 or RAID 6, this can result in noticeable slowdowns, particularly during write-heavy operations. For high-performance environments, such as enterprise-level applications or systems with high I/O demands, relying on software RAID can lead to a decrease in overall system efficiency.

Additionally, software RAID tends to be less reliable in certain scenarios. Since it relies on the operating system and the CPU for RAID management, any issues with the operating system or hardware, such as a system crash or an overloaded CPU, can lead to problems with the RAID array. Furthermore, software RAID typically lacks the advanced features found in hardware RAID solutions, such as hardware-based caching, battery-backed cache, or more sophisticated error handling. While software RAID can handle most basic storage needs, it may not provide the same level of resilience or advanced functionality as hardware RAID.

On the other hand, hardware RAID uses a dedicated RAID controller card or an integrated RAID solution on the motherboard to manage the RAID array. This controller is responsible for all RAID-related tasks, including striping, mirroring, and parity calculations, offloading these operations from the system's CPU. Because the RAID controller handles the RAID functions independently of the operating system, hardware RAID systems tend to offer better performance and reliability, especially for demanding applications that require high throughput and low latency.

The primary advantage of hardware RAID is its superior performance. Since the RAID controller has its own dedicated processor and memory, it is optimized for handling the complex calculations required by RAID levels such as RAID 5 and RAID 6. This allows hardware RAID systems to provide much faster performance than software RAID, particularly when dealing with high-volume read and write operations. For enterprises and organizations that rely on mission-critical applications and need to ensure high-speed data access, hardware RAID is often the preferred choice, as it guarantees better performance with less strain on the main system resources.

Another key benefit of hardware RAID is its reliability and advanced features. Most hardware RAID controllers come with built-in error handling, automatic rebuild features, and battery-backed cache, which can greatly enhance the reliability of the RAID system. If a drive fails, hardware RAID controllers can often automatically rebuild the array without the need for manual intervention, reducing the risk of data loss and minimizing downtime. Additionally, hardware RAID often supports advanced RAID levels, such as RAID 50 or RAID 60, which are not typically available in software RAID configurations.

Furthermore, hardware RAID provides more robust data protection and fault tolerance than software RAID. Many hardware RAID solutions include features such as hot spares, which allow a replacement drive to automatically take over if a failure occurs, and advanced error-correcting techniques to prevent data corruption. These features are especially important in enterprise environments where data loss or downtime can have significant financial consequences.

However, hardware RAID is not without its drawbacks. One of the major disadvantages is cost. Hardware RAID requires a dedicated RAID controller, which can be expensive, especially for high-end models with advanced features like battery-backed cache and support for multiple RAID levels. Additionally, hardware RAID is generally more complex to configure and manage than software RAID, requiring specialized knowledge of RAID controllers and firmware. In some cases, hardware RAID may also be limited by the specific controller's compatibility with certain disk types or configurations, requiring additional investment in compatible hardware.

Another potential issue with hardware RAID is its lack of flexibility. Since hardware RAID is tied to a specific RAID controller, it is often difficult or impossible to migrate the array to a different system without transferring the entire controller and array setup. This lack of portability can be problematic if the RAID system needs to be upgraded or moved to a new platform. In contrast, software RAID is more flexible, as it is independent of the hardware and can easily be transferred between different systems or configurations.

In terms of data recovery, hardware RAID solutions may offer more efficient ways of rebuilding arrays after a failure, but they can also pose challenges if the RAID controller itself fails. While many hardware

RAID systems include backup and redundancy features, recovering from controller failure can be more complex than with software RAID, especially if the RAID controller is proprietary or no longer supported.

When deciding between software and hardware RAID, the key factors to consider are performance requirements, cost, flexibility, and the level of reliability needed for the specific application. For users who require high-speed performance, advanced features, and better fault tolerance, hardware RAID is typically the better choice. However, for those with limited budgets or simpler storage needs, software RAID offers a cost-effective and flexible solution, especially when high throughput and complex error-handling capabilities are not required. Ultimately, the choice between software and hardware RAID depends on the specific requirements of the system, the available resources, and the trade-offs that the user is willing to make in terms of cost, complexity, and performance.

RAID on SSDs: Performance and Challenges

RAID configurations have been a staple in the world of storage for decades, providing redundancy, performance optimization, and fault tolerance across various types of disk drives. However, with the rapid evolution of storage technologies, particularly with the widespread adoption of solid-state drives (SSDs), traditional RAID configurations face both significant improvements and unique challenges. The performance advantages of SSDs, such as faster read and write speeds, low latency, and durability, have made them an appealing option for modern storage solutions. But when used in RAID arrays, the characteristics of SSDs introduce new complexities that must be carefully considered. RAID on SSDs provides a unique blend of performance benefits and potential challenges, requiring an understanding of how SSDs behave in these configurations and how their characteristics can impact overall system performance.

One of the primary reasons for using SSDs in RAID arrays is their remarkable performance improvement over traditional hard disk drives (HDDs). SSDs use flash memory to store data, which enables them to access and write data at significantly higher speeds compared to the mechanical platters of HDDs. This makes them particularly advantageous in RAID configurations designed for high-performance environments, such as databases, video editing, gaming, or virtualized storage systems. When multiple SSDs are used in RAID, the speed advantages compound, further boosting the overall throughput of the array. For instance, RAID 0, which stripes data across multiple drives, allows for parallel access to different parts of the data, effectively multiplying the performance of a single SSD by the number of drives in the array.

RAID 5 and RAID 6, which provide redundancy through parity, also benefit from the use of SSDs. These RAID levels combine data striping with parity data to ensure that data is protected in the event of a drive failure. When SSDs are used in these RAID configurations, the reduced latency and faster read and write speeds of SSDs can improve the overall performance of the array. The speed with which SSDs can read and write data reduces the performance hit typically associated with parity calculations, allowing RAID 5 and RAID 6 configurations to operate at higher speeds than they would with HDDs. In systems where uptime and performance are critical, using SSDs in RAID arrays can offer both data protection and the speed needed to maintain high levels of performance.

However, while SSDs offer substantial performance improvements over HDDs, they also introduce several challenges when used in RAID arrays. One of the most significant challenges is the wear and tear associated with the limited lifespan of SSDs. Unlike HDDs, which can continue to function reliably for many years, SSDs have a limited number of write cycles before they begin to degrade. Each write to an SSD consumes part of the drive's lifespan, and as the drive reaches its wear limit, the risk of data corruption or failure increases. This phenomenon is known as write endurance, and it can become a critical issue in RAID arrays that experience frequent writes, especially in RAID 5 and RAID 6, where parity information must be updated regularly.

When SSDs are used in RAID 5 or RAID 6 configurations, the parity updates required for each write operation can lead to significant wear on the drives, especially if the system is highly write-intensive. This issue is exacerbated in SSD-based RAID arrays because the drives will eventually begin to fail once their write endurance is reached. The implications of this can be far-reaching, as the failure of a single SSD in a RAID 5 or RAID 6 array can lead to degraded performance, data loss, or the need for costly drive replacements and array rebuilds. To mitigate this risk, many modern SSDs are designed with wear-leveling algorithms that distribute writes evenly across the drive, but even these mechanisms cannot prevent all instances of wear over time.

Another challenge that arises when using SSDs in RAID configurations is the issue of over-provisioning. SSDs generally come with built-in spare memory cells that are used to replace damaged cells as the drive wears out. However, the level of over-provisioning in SSDs varies widely depending on the manufacturer and model. When SSDs are used in RAID arrays, the potential for uneven wear across multiple drives can lead to some drives reaching their wear limit faster than others. This imbalance can cause issues with RAID performance and reliability, as the array may be forced to rebuild using a drive that has a significantly shorter remaining lifespan than the others. This makes it crucial to carefully monitor the health of each drive in the array, which can add an extra layer of complexity to SSD-based RAID systems.

Another factor to consider when using SSDs in RAID arrays is the potential for data retention issues. SSDs rely on electrical charges to store data, and as the drive ages or is exposed to heat and other environmental factors, the ability of the drive to retain data can diminish. In a RAID configuration, this issue can be compounded if one of the SSDs in the array begins to degrade or lose its ability to retain data. In traditional HDD-based RAID systems, data is typically written to the disk in a linear fashion, making it easier to recover from drive failures. In contrast, the complexity of NAND flash memory and its wear patterns can make data recovery in SSD-based RAID systems more challenging, particularly if multiple drives are involved.

Additionally, while SSDs excel in random access performance, they may not always perform as well in sequential write-heavy tasks compared to HDDs. In RAID configurations that involve extensive write operations, such as RAID 5 or RAID 6, where parity data is calculated and written to the disk frequently, SSDs may face challenges in maintaining consistent performance levels. This is because SSDs have limitations when it comes to handling sustained write operations over extended periods, particularly in systems with many drives that must synchronize data and parity information. Consequently, RAID arrays that leverage SSDs for high-speed storage may experience some inconsistency in performance if write-heavy operations dominate the workload.

The cost of SSDs is another consideration when implementing them in RAID arrays. SSDs are significantly more expensive than traditional HDDs, and using them in RAID configurations can lead to higher upfront costs. While the performance benefits may justify the price for certain applications, the increased cost of SSD-based storage can be a limiting factor for many organizations or individuals seeking cost-effective solutions for large-scale storage. This cost-benefit ratio must be carefully considered, especially in environments where raw storage capacity is prioritized over performance.

Despite these challenges, the combination of SSDs and RAID configurations offers compelling benefits, particularly in high-performance applications where speed and reliability are paramount. The use of SSDs in RAID arrays can result in dramatically faster read and write speeds, improved system responsiveness, and reduced latency. For environments that require constant uptime, such as database systems, virtualization platforms, and high-performance computing environments, SSD-based RAID arrays offer significant advantages over traditional HDD-based systems.

As SSD technology continues to evolve, many of the challenges associated with using SSDs in RAID arrays, such as wear endurance and data retention issues, will likely diminish. Newer SSD models with enhanced durability, better wear-leveling algorithms, and improved power-loss protection will continue to make SSD-based RAID solutions more reliable and cost-effective. Moreover, advancements in RAID controller technology and storage management software will help mitigate some of the performance bottlenecks and reliability concerns that currently exist. As these technologies mature, SSDs in RAID configurations will become an even more attractive option for users who require both high performance and robust data protection.

The Importance of Redundancy in RAID Configurations

Redundancy in RAID configurations is one of the cornerstones of modern data storage systems. The principle of redundancy revolves around the idea of creating copies or employing algorithms to ensure that, in the event of a hardware failure, critical data remains accessible and intact. Redundancy is particularly important in enterprise environments, where system uptime, data integrity, and business continuity are critical. The integration of redundancy into RAID (Redundant Array of Independent Disks) configurations addresses the fundamental problem of single points of failure in traditional data storage methods, significantly improving data reliability and availability.

At the heart of RAID technology lies the ability to store data across multiple physical drives, with the specific configuration determined by the selected RAID level. The redundancy in RAID is achieved through a combination of techniques such as data mirroring, parity, and striping, which help mitigate the risk of data loss in the event of a drive failure. Different RAID levels offer varying degrees of redundancy, from the simple mirroring of data in RAID 1 to the more complex parity-based redundancy in RAID 5 and RAID 6. Each configuration provides a unique approach to balancing performance, capacity, and fault tolerance.

One of the most widely used methods of providing redundancy in RAID is data mirroring. In RAID 1, data is duplicated on two or more drives, ensuring that an exact copy of the data exists in case one drive fails. This means that if one drive experiences a hardware failure, the system can continue to operate using the mirrored copy of the data from the second drive. RAID 1 offers excellent redundancy but sacrifices storage efficiency since the data is duplicated. However, it is ideal for situations where data protection is the highest priority, and performance or capacity is secondary.

Another commonly used technique for achieving redundancy is parity. Parity-based RAID levels, such as RAID 5 and RAID 6, use a more sophisticated method of data protection by distributing parity data across the drives in the array. Parity data is essentially a mathematical calculation that can be used to reconstruct lost data in the event of a drive failure. In RAID 5, data is striped across multiple drives, and the parity information is distributed across all the drives, providing protection against the failure of a single drive. RAID 6 takes this further by using two sets of parity data, allowing it to tolerate the simultaneous failure of two drives without data loss. While parity-based RAID levels offer a more storage-efficient solution than mirroring, they introduce some performance overhead, especially in write-intensive applications, due to the need to calculate and update the parity data.

The key benefit of redundancy in RAID configurations is the protection it provides against data loss. Hard drives, like any other mechanical component, are susceptible to failure over time. In traditional single-drive systems, a failure results in the complete loss of the data stored on that drive. In contrast, RAID with redundancy ensures that if one drive fails, the data can still be accessed from the other drives in the array. This is particularly crucial for businesses and organizations that rely on constant access to their data. For example, in industries like healthcare, finance, or e-commerce, data loss can have serious consequences, ranging from regulatory penalties to loss of customer trust. By incorporating redundancy into RAID configurations, organizations can safeguard their critical data and minimize the impact of hardware failures.

Another important aspect of redundancy in RAID is its ability to enhance system uptime. In environments where high availability is a requirement, RAID redundancy ensures that data remains accessible even in the event of a drive failure. This is particularly valuable for online services, data centers, and cloud storage providers, where any downtime can result in significant financial losses and customer dissatisfaction. With RAID configurations that include redundancy, systems can continue to operate seamlessly while the failed drive is replaced, and the array is rebuilt. This failover capability ensures that businesses can maintain operations without the need for extended outages, providing a higher level of service to end users.

While redundancy in RAID configurations provides significant protection against drive failure, it is not a substitute for a comprehensive data backup strategy. RAID redundancy ensures that data remains available and intact in the event of hardware failure, but it does not protect against other types of data loss, such as accidental deletion, corruption, or malicious attacks. For example, if a user unintentionally deletes critical files or if ransomware infects the system, the RAID array's redundancy will not prevent the loss of that data. This is why it is essential to pair RAID configurations with regular backups to ensure complete protection against all forms of data loss.

The importance of redundancy also extends to ensuring data integrity. In environments where data corruption is a concern, RAID can help prevent the loss of data integrity by providing multiple copies of the same data or by using parity to reconstruct lost or corrupted data. RAID 1, for example, ensures that every bit of data is mirrored, offering a safeguard against accidental corruption or modification. RAID 5 and RAID 6, with their parity-based approach, offer similar protection while balancing storage efficiency and fault tolerance. In critical applications such as databases or file systems, where data integrity is paramount, RAID redundancy helps ensure that data is consistent and reliable, even in the face of hardware failure.

While redundancy in RAID systems provides significant benefits, it is important to recognize that it is not without trade-offs. RAID configurations that use redundancy, such as RAID 1, RAID 5, or RAID 6, often come with increased costs due to the need for additional drives and the associated storage overhead. RAID 1, for example, requires twice the number of drives to store the same amount of data, while RAID 5 and RAID 6 use parity data, which also reduces the usable storage capacity. Additionally, redundancy introduces complexity in terms of system management. While RAID 1 is relatively straightforward, RAID 5 and RAID 6 require careful monitoring of the parity data and the array's health to ensure that data is protected and rebuilds occur smoothly in the event of a drive failure.

Redundancy also impacts performance. While RAID 1 offers excellent fault tolerance and fast read speeds, its write performance may be slower than other RAID levels due to the need to duplicate data across multiple drives. RAID 5 and RAID 6 offer better storage efficiency and improved read performance, but the parity calculations required for write operations can slow down write speeds, especially in high-write environments. The performance overhead introduced by redundancy must be considered when selecting the appropriate RAID configuration for a given application.

Redundancy in RAID configurations is an essential feature that enhances data protection, availability, and integrity. It helps mitigate the risks associated with hardware failure, ensuring that critical data remains accessible and intact even in the event of a drive failure. By incorporating redundancy into their storage systems, organizations can protect their data, minimize downtime, and ensure the continuity of their operations. However, as with any storage solution, it is important to carefully weigh the trade-offs between redundancy, performance, storage efficiency, and cost to determine the best RAID configuration for a particular environment or use case.

RAID in Enterprise Storage Solutions

RAID technology has become an essential component in modern enterprise storage solutions. As businesses grow and data storage needs expand, organizations require systems that not only provide large amounts of storage but also ensure data availability, integrity, and protection. RAID, which stands for Redundant Array of Independent Disks, addresses these critical requirements by combining multiple physical hard drives or solid-state drives into a single logical unit, offering significant benefits in performance, fault tolerance, and scalability. In enterprise environments, where uptime, data security, and performance are of paramount importance, RAID is crucial for supporting a range of applications, from databases to virtualization and cloud storage.

The implementation of RAID in enterprise storage solutions allows for increased storage capacity while reducing the risk of data loss due to hardware failure. With traditional single-disk storage systems, a single point of failure could result in catastrophic data loss. RAID, by contrast, incorporates redundancy through various methods such as mirroring, striping, and parity to protect against drive failures. Depending on the chosen RAID level, different degrees of redundancy and performance are provided. For example, RAID 1, which uses mirroring, ensures that every piece of data is duplicated across two drives, offering excellent protection against data loss. RAID 5 and RAID 6, on the other hand, use parity and striping to provide fault tolerance with greater storage efficiency, making them popular choices in environments where both data protection and storage efficiency are important.

RAID's role in enterprise storage solutions is particularly important in environments that handle large amounts of data or require high availability. For instance, RAID 10, a combination of RAID 1 and RAID 0, is often deployed in high-performance applications such as online transaction processing (OLTP) systems or virtualized environments. RAID 10 combines the performance benefits of striping (RAID 0) with the redundancy of mirroring (RAID 1), making it an ideal choice for businesses that require both high-speed access to data and a safeguard against drive failure. This configuration is typically used in enterprise settings where system performance cannot be compromised, and where data protection is a priority, as it offers the best of both worlds: fast read/write speeds and a high level of redundancy.

Another widely used RAID level in enterprise environments is RAID 5, which offers a good balance between performance, fault tolerance, and storage capacity. In RAID 5, data is striped across multiple drives, and parity information is distributed across all the drives in the array. The parity data allows for the recovery of lost data if a drive fails, and it provides fault tolerance without requiring duplication of data as in RAID 1. This makes RAID 5 a cost-effective solution for environments that require redundancy but cannot afford the overhead associated with full data mirroring. RAID 5 is particularly popular in environments that demand large storage capacity, such as file servers or backup systems, where data is being constantly accessed and written to.

RAID 6 extends the concept of RAID 5 by adding a second set of parity data, which allows it to tolerate the simultaneous failure of two drives. This added redundancy makes RAID 6 an attractive option for mission-critical applications where data availability must be guaranteed, even in the event of multiple drive failures. However, RAID 6 does come with a performance penalty due to the additional parity calculations that must be performed for each write operation. Despite this, its ability to provide extra protection against data loss while maintaining reasonable performance makes it suitable for enterprise environments that require maximum data protection, such as in data centers or large-scale cloud storage systems.

In addition to fault tolerance and redundancy, RAID also plays a significant role in enhancing performance in enterprise storage solutions. Data striping, which is a key component in RAID 0, RAID 5, and RAID 10, allows for faster read and write operations by distributing data across multiple drives. When data is spread across several disks, multiple read and write requests can be processed simultaneously, significantly increasing throughput. This is especially important in environments with high I/O demand, such as database applications or media editing systems, where large amounts of data need to be accessed quickly.

RAID also contributes to scalability, another important factor in enterprise storage systems. As an organization's storage needs grow, RAID configurations can be expanded to accommodate additional drives without the need to overhaul the entire system. For example, in a RAID 5 setup, additional drives can be added to the array, increasing both capacity and performance while maintaining the same level of redundancy. This flexibility allows businesses to scale their storage infrastructure over time, ensuring that their systems can grow in tandem with their data requirements. Similarly, RAID 6's additional parity ensures that scalability is achieved without compromising data protection, which is crucial for environments where data integrity is non-negotiable.

One of the most significant challenges when implementing RAID in enterprise storage solutions is the complexity of managing and maintaining the RAID array. RAID systems require careful monitoring to ensure that all drives are functioning correctly, as a failure in one drive can impact the performance or redundancy of the entire array. RAID systems, particularly those with more complex configurations like RAID 5 and RAID 6, require constant attention to drive health, parity calculations, and rebuilding procedures in the event of a failure. The rebuild process can be particularly resource-intensive and time-consuming, as it involves reconstructing data from the remaining drives using parity information. This can place a significant load on the system, potentially affecting performance during the rebuild process.

Another challenge of RAID in enterprise storage solutions is the cost associated with maintaining the necessary hardware. While RAID provides redundancy and performance benefits, it also requires additional drives, RAID controllers, and infrastructure to operate efficiently. This can result in higher upfront costs compared to non-RAID configurations, particularly in larger systems. Furthermore, RAID configurations with higher levels of redundancy, such as RAID 6 or RAID 10, often require more disks, increasing both the initial investment and the ongoing maintenance costs.

Despite these challenges, RAID remains an essential technology for modern enterprise storage solutions. It provides a reliable and flexible way to manage data, offering both performance enhancements and fault tolerance in one package. In industries where uptime is critical and data loss cannot be tolerated, RAID plays a central role in ensuring that storage systems meet the rigorous demands of today's data-driven environments. Whether through simple mirroring for redundancy, or more complex configurations like RAID 5 and RAID 6 that balance performance with fault tolerance, RAID offers businesses the ability to optimize their storage infrastructure, protect critical data, and scale their operations as needed.

As the need for faster, more reliable storage continues to grow, RAID technology will continue to evolve and adapt to new challenges. With the rise of solid-state drives (SSDs) and the growing importance of cloud storage, RAID configurations are becoming increasingly relevant in addressing the high-performance and high-redundancy needs of modern enterprise environments. The ability to leverage RAID in enterprise storage systems ensures that businesses can remain agile and resilient, even in the face of evolving technological landscapes.

Understanding RAID Controllers

RAID controllers are fundamental components in any RAID-based storage system, acting as the bridge between the operating system and the physical storage devices. A RAID controller is a specialized hardware or software solution designed to manage the distribution of data across multiple disks, ensuring that the data is stored according to the chosen RAID configuration. By handling the complexity of data striping, mirroring, and parity calculations, RAID controllers play a crucial role in improving the performance, redundancy, and reliability of storage systems. Understanding how RAID controllers work, their different types, and their impact on overall system performance is essential for anyone involved in configuring or managing RAID-based storage solutions.

The primary function of a RAID controller is to coordinate the activities of multiple storage devices in a RAID array. In a RAID system, data is distributed across multiple disks, often to enhance performance (by striping data across multiple drives) or to provide redundancy (through mirroring or parity). The RAID controller is responsible for managing how data is written and read from these drives, ensuring that the data is consistent and secure, even in the event of a drive failure. For instance, in RAID 1, the controller will mirror the data across two drives, while in RAID 5, the controller will distribute data and parity across three or more disks.

There are two primary types of RAID controllers: hardware RAID controllers and software RAID controllers. Each type has its own advantages and disadvantages, depending on the specific needs of the system. Hardware RAID controllers are dedicated physical devices that handle all of the RAID functions independently of the host computer's CPU. These controllers have their own processors and memory, which allows them to offload the RAID processing workload from the main system, improving performance, especially in write-intensive applications. Hardware RAID controllers are often used in enterprise environments, where high availability and performance are critical. They offer advanced features, such as battery-backed cache, hot spare management, and enhanced error recovery, making them well-suited for mission-critical applications.

Software RAID controllers, on the other hand, use the host computer's CPU and system memory to manage RAID operations. This type of RAID is often built into the operating system or can be implemented through third-party software. Software RAID does not require any dedicated hardware, making it a more cost-effective solution for smaller environments or less demanding workloads. However, because the CPU is responsible for managing the RAID functions, software

RAID can place additional load on the system, particularly when dealing with complex RAID configurations like RAID 5 or RAID 6, which require parity calculations. Despite this, software RAID has its place in many systems where performance is not as critical, and its flexibility and ease of use make it a popular choice in personal computers or small office setups.

RAID controllers, whether hardware or software, can support a wide range of RAID levels, each designed to meet specific storage needs. The choice of RAID level depends on factors such as the required balance between performance and redundancy, the amount of storage capacity needed, and the type of applications the system will run. RAID 0, for instance, is a simple striping configuration that offers improved performance but does not provide any redundancy. A RAID controller will manage the distribution of data across the drives, ensuring that data is written and read efficiently. RAID 1, which mirrors data across two drives, offers redundancy by ensuring that an identical copy of the data is available on both disks. RAID 5 and RAID 6 offer a combination of striping and parity for data protection, with RAID 5 requiring at least three drives and RAID 6 requiring at least four drives to distribute both data and parity information across the array.

Hardware RAID controllers often provide additional features that enhance the performance and reliability of the RAID array. For example, many high-end hardware RAID controllers come equipped with onboard cache memory, which temporarily stores data before it is written to the drives. This cache helps improve write speeds by allowing the controller to quickly store data in memory, then flush it to the drives later. This can significantly enhance the overall performance of the RAID system, especially for applications that involve a high volume of write operations, such as databases or video editing. Battery-backed cache is another feature found in some hardware RAID controllers, providing power to the cache memory during a power failure. This ensures that data is not lost if the system loses power during write operations, thereby improving data integrity.

Another key advantage of hardware RAID controllers is their ability to support advanced features like hot spares and automatic rebuilds. A hot spare is a drive that is kept in standby mode and can automatically replace a failed drive in the RAID array without user intervention.

When a drive fails, the RAID controller immediately begins rebuilding the array using the hot spare, reducing downtime and maintaining redundancy in the system. Automatic rebuilds are crucial in enterprise environments, where uptime is critical, as they help restore the array to a fully protected state without requiring manual intervention. These features, along with the controller's ability to manage drive failures and monitor drive health, make hardware RAID controllers a highly reliable choice for mission-critical storage systems.

The choice of RAID controller can also affect the scalability of the storage solution. In enterprise environments, where storage needs often grow over time, a scalable RAID controller is essential. Many hardware RAID controllers are designed to support a large number of drives and can be expanded by adding additional RAID controller cards or connecting external enclosures. This scalability ensures that organizations can easily increase their storage capacity as their data requirements grow, without the need to replace the entire storage infrastructure. Additionally, hardware RAID controllers often come with management software that allows system administrators to monitor the health of the array, configure RAID levels, and perform diagnostic checks to prevent failures.

While hardware RAID controllers offer significant benefits in terms of performance and advanced features, software RAID solutions are often preferred for their flexibility and cost-effectiveness. Software RAID is typically easier to configure and can be managed directly through the operating system, making it accessible to users with limited technical expertise. Furthermore, software RAID does not require the additional expense of a dedicated hardware controller, making it a more affordable option for smaller systems or less demanding applications. Software RAID also benefits from its flexibility, as it can work with a wide range of hardware configurations and can be easily reconfigured if the storage needs change.

However, software RAID does come with certain limitations. One of the primary drawbacks of software RAID is that it relies on the system's CPU and memory to handle RAID operations. This means that performance can be impacted by the processing power and resources of the host system, especially when dealing with more complex RAID configurations. RAID 5 and RAID 6, for example, require significant computational resources to manage parity data, which can place a heavy load on the CPU, resulting in slower performance compared to hardware RAID.

RAID controllers are indispensable components in enterprise storage solutions, offering a crucial role in managing and optimizing storage systems. Whether through hardware or software, RAID controllers provide the necessary tools to improve data redundancy, performance, and scalability, making them vital for businesses that require reliable and high-performance storage infrastructure. The choice of RAID controller—hardware or software—depends on factors such as the scale of the system, performance requirements, budget, and the complexity of the storage solution. Each type of RAID controller brings its own set of benefits and challenges, and understanding these differences is key to selecting the right solution for any enterprise storage environment.

Hot Spares and Their Role in RAID

Hot spares are an important feature in many RAID configurations, playing a crucial role in ensuring the continued availability and reliability of data in enterprise storage systems. A hot spare is an additional drive that remains idle and is not part of the RAID array's active data storage under normal conditions. Its primary function is to automatically take over for a failed drive in the RAID array, allowing the array to continue operating without significant downtime or data loss. This feature is particularly important in environments where data availability is critical, and even brief periods of downtime can lead to significant disruptions or financial losses.

In RAID configurations that include redundancy, such as RAID 1, RAID 5, and RAID 6, the role of hot spares is to provide a seamless failover mechanism when a drive within the array fails. For example, in a RAID 5 array, data is striped across multiple drives, and parity information is distributed to provide fault tolerance. If one drive fails, the array can continue to operate with degraded performance, but the data is at risk until the failed drive is replaced. This is where a hot spare comes into play. The hot spare is automatically integrated into the array as a replacement for the failed drive, and the RAID controller begins the rebuild process, reconstructing the lost data using the parity information. This allows the array to return to a fully redundant state without requiring manual intervention, significantly reducing downtime and maintaining system reliability.

The inclusion of hot spares in RAID arrays helps mitigate the risks associated with drive failure, which is one of the primary concerns in storage systems. Hard drives, especially mechanical drives, are prone to failure due to factors such as age, wear and tear, and power surges. In a RAID configuration without hot spares, when a drive fails, the system enters a degraded mode, and the user must manually replace the failed drive. This process can take time, during which the array is at risk. During this period, the remaining drives in the array are under increased stress as they handle the additional workload. The probability of a second drive failure, while the array is in a degraded state, increases the risk of data loss. A hot spare reduces this risk by allowing the failed drive to be replaced automatically, ensuring the array is quickly restored to full redundancy.

Hot spares can be particularly useful in large-scale storage systems, where the number of drives in use increases the likelihood of failure. In such systems, manually monitoring the health of every individual drive and promptly replacing any failures can be a cumbersome and error-prone task. A hot spare eliminates the need for constant manual intervention, providing an automatic and efficient solution to drive failures. This is especially valuable in enterprise environments, such as data centers, cloud storage providers, and large-scale file servers, where the demand for continuous uptime is high and the risks associated with downtime are significant.

The effectiveness of hot spares in RAID systems is enhanced by their ability to work in conjunction with advanced RAID controllers. RAID controllers typically include monitoring features that track the health and status of each drive in the array, as well as the ability to automatically detect when a drive fails. When a drive is detected as faulty, the RAID controller automatically activates the hot spare and begins the rebuilding process without requiring any user interaction. This automatic failover capability ensures that the system can continue to function smoothly, even in the event of a failure.

One of the key advantages of using hot spares is that they can reduce the time it takes to restore redundancy in the array. In traditional RAID systems without hot spares, when a drive fails, the user must first replace the faulty drive manually, and then the RAID system must rebuild the array. This can be a time-consuming process, especially in large arrays with large amounts of data. By contrast, with a hot spare, the replacement process is automated, and the system can begin rebuilding the data immediately, often resulting in faster recovery times. This helps minimize downtime, which is essential for businesses that rely on continuous access to their data.

However, while hot spares offer significant benefits, they also come with some considerations. One potential drawback is the cost of maintaining extra drives. A hot spare requires the allocation of a spare drive that will not be used for normal storage operations until a failure occurs. This means that businesses need to invest in additional hardware to maintain hot spares, which can increase the overall cost of the RAID array. In some cases, organizations may choose to use a hot spare only in high-priority systems where data availability is critical, while opting for a less expensive solution in other systems where downtime can be tolerated.

Another consideration is the impact on storage capacity. Since hot spares are idle unless a failure occurs, they do not contribute to the usable storage capacity of the RAID array. In RAID configurations that require a large amount of storage, such as RAID 5 or RAID 6, the cost of dedicating a drive to act as a hot spare may be viewed as a trade-off between capacity and data protection. Additionally, when the hot spare is used to replace a failed drive, it takes the place of one of the drives in the array, which temporarily reduces the overall available capacity until the rebuild process is completed.

The rebuild process, while essential to restoring redundancy, can also be resource-intensive. During the rebuild, data is reconstructed from the remaining drives using parity information, which can place a significant load on the system's I/O performance. This can result in slower read and write operations until the rebuild process is finished. The presence of a hot spare helps reduce downtime during this process, but it is still important to consider the potential performance impact, particularly in write-heavy environments. In some cases, systems with hot spares may use techniques such as prioritizing read over write operations during the rebuild to minimize the impact on performance.

The use of hot spares in RAID systems also raises the importance of proactive maintenance and monitoring. While the automatic failover to a hot spare helps to address drive failures quickly, it is still important to ensure that the system is functioning optimally. RAID controllers with advanced monitoring capabilities can alert system administrators when a drive is nearing failure, allowing them to take preventive action before a failure occurs. Regularly checking the health of the RAID array and performing maintenance tasks, such as updating firmware and replacing aging drives, can help extend the lifespan of the system and ensure the continued reliability of the RAID array.

Hot spares are an invaluable tool for improving the reliability and uptime of RAID systems, especially in enterprise environments where data availability is critical. By automating the process of replacing failed drives, hot spares minimize downtime, reduce the risk of data loss, and allow for faster recovery times. However, their use requires careful consideration of factors such as cost, storage capacity, and performance impact during rebuilds. When implemented correctly, hot spares can significantly enhance the reliability of RAID configurations, making them a key component of any enterprise storage solution.

Rebuilding a Failed RAID Array

Rebuilding a failed RAID array is a critical process in ensuring the continuity of data storage systems. RAID arrays are widely used in both consumer and enterprise environments to provide redundancy and improve performance, but like any technology, they are susceptible to failure. A failed RAID array can result in a significant disruption of operations, especially if the system is being used for critical data storage or high-performance applications. The rebuilding process aims to restore the array to its full capacity and functionality after a drive failure, ensuring that the data remains accessible and protected. However, the process can be complex, time-consuming, and resource-intensive, requiring careful attention and a structured approach.

When a drive fails in a RAID array, the first step is to assess the type of RAID configuration being used and the extent of the failure. Depending on the RAID level, the array may still function in a degraded mode, meaning that one or more drives have failed but the system can continue to operate. In configurations like RAID 1, RAID 5, or RAID 6, data redundancy is built into the system, and the array can still function even with a drive failure. However, while the array is still operational, it is not fully redundant, and the system remains vulnerable to further failure until the array is rebuilt. If a second drive fails before the rebuild is complete, data loss may occur, especially in non-mirrored RAID levels like RAID 5 or RAID 6.

The first step in rebuilding a failed RAID array is to replace the failed drive with a new or functional one. In a mirrored RAID 1 setup, for example, this means replacing the failed drive with a new one that is identical in size or greater. In RAID 5 and RAID 6, the new drive will be used to rebuild the data lost from the failed drive using the parity information stored on the remaining drives. In some cases, the RAID controller may automatically detect the failed drive and prompt the system to begin the rebuilding process once the new drive is inserted into the array. This automatic process typically occurs in hardware RAID configurations, where the controller can manage the reconstruction of the array.

However, in software RAID configurations, the rebuild process is generally initiated manually. The system administrator must ensure that the replacement drive is properly recognized by the operating system and is integrated into the RAID array. This typically involves using RAID management tools or the operating system's native disk management utilities to initiate the rebuild. For example, in Linux systems, the "mdadm" utility is often used to manage and rebuild RAID arrays, while Windows Server environments use built-in RAID management features to rebuild arrays. It is essential to verify that the new drive is fully functional before starting the rebuild process, as using a faulty or incompatible drive can lead to further issues.

During the rebuild process, the RAID controller or software utility will begin to reconstruct the lost data on the new drive. This is done using the remaining data in the array and, in the case of RAID 5 or RAID 6, the parity information that was distributed across the other drives.

Parity data serves as a form of error correction, and it allows the system to reconstruct data from a failed drive without data loss. The rebuild process may take several hours or even days, depending on the size of the drives and the amount of data in the array. While the rebuild is in progress, system performance may degrade, as the remaining drives are tasked with both maintaining the array's operation and reconstructing the lost data.

It is crucial to closely monitor the rebuild process to ensure that it progresses without issues. RAID controllers and software utilities often provide status updates on the rebuild process, showing the percentage of data that has been successfully reconstructed. During this time, it is advisable to avoid heavy read/write operations on the array to reduce the load and minimize the chances of another drive failure during the rebuild. Administrators should also keep an eye on the health of the remaining drives, as any additional failures could result in permanent data loss, particularly in RAID 5 and RAID 6 configurations, which can tolerate only one or two drive failures, respectively.

Once the rebuild process is complete, the RAID array should return to full redundancy, and the new drive will be fully integrated into the system. At this point, the array will be restored to its original capacity, and the system will be protected against future failures. It is important to verify that the rebuilt drive is functioning correctly by running diagnostics on the array and checking for any errors or inconsistencies. Additionally, administrators should ensure that the RAID configuration is properly re-synced and that all data is correctly mirrored or striped, depending on the RAID level being used.

However, while the rebuild process restores redundancy and data protection to the array, it does not solve the underlying issue that caused the original failure. It is essential to investigate the root cause of the drive failure and take steps to prevent future issues. Common causes of RAID array failures include power surges, mechanical failure of drives, or issues with the RAID controller itself. For example, if the failure was caused by an issue with the RAID controller, it may be necessary to replace or upgrade the controller to prevent future failures. Additionally, regular maintenance and monitoring of the drives and RAID system can help identify potential issues before they lead to failures, allowing administrators to replace aging or failing drives proactively.

Another important consideration when rebuilding a failed RAID array is data recovery. In some cases, the data on the failed drive may be partially or fully recoverable, even if the RAID system is not able to rebuild it. If a RAID array experiences multiple drive failures or if the rebuild process fails, data recovery services may be required to retrieve lost information. Specialized data recovery tools and techniques are used to extract data from damaged or corrupted drives, but this process can be costly and time-consuming. To minimize the risk of data loss, regular backups should always be implemented in conjunction with RAID arrays, as backups provide an additional layer of protection in case of catastrophic failure.

Rebuilding a failed RAID array is a crucial process for restoring data availability and protecting against future failures. While the process can be straightforward in some cases, it requires careful attention and planning to ensure that it is done correctly and efficiently. Ensuring the health of the replacement drive, monitoring the rebuild process, and investigating the cause of the failure are essential steps in the recovery process. With proper management and proactive maintenance, RAID systems can continue to provide reliable, fault-tolerant storage solutions, even in the face of hardware failures.

RAID and Backup: Complementary Technologies

RAID (Redundant Array of Independent Disks) and data backup are two essential components of modern data protection strategies. While both technologies are designed to ensure the availability and integrity of data, they serve different purposes and are best used in tandem to provide a robust solution for safeguarding critical information. RAID offers redundancy and improves performance by distributing data across multiple disks, while backups provide a separate copy of data that can be restored in the event of data loss or system failure. Together, RAID and backup create a multi-layered approach to data security, offering protection against both hardware failure and user error.

RAID is primarily used for fault tolerance, ensuring that data remains accessible even in the event of a drive failure. In RAID configurations such as RAID 1, RAID 5, or RAID 6, data is either mirrored or striped with parity across multiple disks. This redundancy allows the system to continue operating even if one or more drives fail, without risking data loss. RAID 1, for example, mirrors data on two drives, meaning that if one drive fails, the system can continue to access the data from the second drive. RAID 5 and RAID 6 provide a similar level of fault tolerance but with more storage efficiency, as they use parity data distributed across the array to rebuild lost data when a drive fails. By ensuring that data is still accessible even after a hardware failure, RAID offers a layer of protection against system downtime and data loss.

While RAID provides fault tolerance and continuous access to data in the event of a drive failure, it is not a comprehensive data protection solution on its own. RAID arrays are vulnerable to certain types of data loss that RAID cannot prevent, such as accidental deletion, file corruption, or malicious attacks. For instance, if a user accidentally deletes critical files or if ransomware encrypts the data, RAID will not be able to recover those files, as the system will simply mirror or distribute the corrupted data across the array. In these cases, a backup is the only way to restore the lost or corrupted data to its previous state.

Data backup is designed to complement RAID by providing an external copy of the data that can be restored in case of data loss, whether it is caused by human error, hardware failure, or a security breach. Backups are typically stored separately from the primary storage system, either on external drives, network-attached storage (NAS), or in the cloud. This separation ensures that if the RAID array is compromised, the backup remains intact and can be used to recover the lost data. Unlike RAID, which is focused on preventing data loss due to hardware failure, backups are designed to protect against all types of data loss, including logical errors and user mistakes.

One of the key benefits of using RAID and backup together is the ability to ensure business continuity in the face of disasters or system failures. RAID can maintain the availability of data during hardware failures, ensuring that critical operations are not disrupted while the system is being repaired or the failed drive is replaced. However, RAID does not protect against data loss from other causes, such as file corruption, accidental deletion, or cyberattacks. Backups, on the other hand, can restore data lost due to these factors, providing an additional layer of protection and ensuring that the organization can recover from a wide range of data loss scenarios. When combined, RAID and backup systems create a comprehensive data protection strategy that addresses both hardware and logical data loss.

Another important advantage of using RAID and backup together is the ability to optimize recovery times. RAID systems typically offer fast recovery from hardware failures, as the data can be reconstructed from the remaining drives in the array. However, in more complex situations, such as data corruption or catastrophic system failure, RAID alone may not be sufficient to restore the system to its full state. In these cases, backups are essential for quickly restoring the system to its last known good configuration. By regularly backing up data and combining this with the redundancy provided by RAID, organizations can ensure that they can recover their systems quickly and minimize downtime, even in the face of unexpected disruptions.

Moreover, RAID and backup can be implemented in various combinations to meet the specific needs of different environments. In small-scale environments, such as home offices or small businesses, a simple RAID 1 array, which mirrors data across two drives, can provide redundancy while local backups on an external hard drive or cloud storage can ensure that data is protected from accidental deletion or corruption. In larger, more complex enterprise environments, a combination of RAID 5 or RAID 6 with offsite backups or cloud-based solutions can provide both high availability and long-term data preservation. In these cases, RAID ensures that the system remains operational during hardware failures, while offsite backups ensure that data can be restored in the event of a disaster, such as fire, theft, or a cyberattack.

Despite the critical role RAID and backup systems play in data protection, there are challenges to effectively implementing and managing both technologies. One common challenge is the cost associated with maintaining both RAID arrays and backup systems.

RAID requires additional hard drives to provide redundancy, and as the number of drives increases, so does the cost of the system. Similarly, backup systems require additional storage infrastructure, whether it be on physical disks, network storage, or cloud-based solutions. For organizations with large volumes of data, these costs can add up quickly. However, the investment in RAID and backup is typically outweighed by the protection they provide against data loss and downtime.

Another challenge is ensuring that backup systems are regularly updated and maintained. A backup that is not regularly updated is essentially useless, as it may not reflect the most recent changes in the data. Organizations must implement regular backup schedules, ensuring that the backup systems are up-to-date and capable of recovering the latest versions of data. Additionally, it is important to periodically test backups to ensure that they can be restored successfully. Without regular testing, businesses may find themselves in a situation where they are unable to recover their data, rendering the backup system ineffective.

While RAID and backup serve different functions in data protection, their complementary roles make them indispensable for ensuring the safety and availability of critical data. RAID offers fault tolerance and ensures that data remains accessible in the event of hardware failure, while backups provide a safeguard against all types of data loss, including human error, corruption, and cyber threats. When implemented together, these technologies create a robust and reliable data protection strategy, helping organizations to minimize the risk of data loss and maintain business continuity even in the face of unexpected disruptions. For organizations that rely on their data for daily operations, combining RAID with regular backups is a best practice that provides both peace of mind and the ability to quickly recover from unforeseen challenges.

RAID Expansion and Migration Strategies

As organizations grow and data storage needs evolve, managing and expanding RAID systems becomes a critical aspect of IT infrastructure management. RAID expansion and migration strategies allow businesses to scale their storage systems effectively without disrupting operations or compromising data integrity. These strategies are designed to accommodate increasing storage demands while maintaining optimal performance, fault tolerance, and reliability. Expanding a RAID array involves adding more drives to an existing configuration, while migration refers to the process of changing or upgrading the RAID level or moving data to a different storage platform or technology. Both processes are crucial for adapting to changing business requirements and ensuring that storage systems remain efficient and scalable.

One of the primary motivations for RAID expansion is the need to increase storage capacity. As businesses accumulate more data, the existing storage solutions may become inadequate to meet the growing demand. RAID configurations, particularly those with high redundancy such as RAID 1, RAID 5, or RAID 6, can be expanded by adding additional drives to the array. In a RAID 5 array, for example, adding another drive can increase the overall storage capacity while maintaining data protection through parity. RAID 6, with its dual parity, can also be expanded in a similar fashion, providing additional storage capacity without sacrificing redundancy. Expanding a RAID array allows businesses to scale their storage solutions without needing to replace existing drives, making it a cost-effective way to increase capacity.

However, expanding RAID systems is not without its challenges. One of the main considerations during expansion is the balance between performance and redundancy. While adding drives to a RAID array increases storage capacity, it can also affect performance, particularly in configurations like RAID 5 or RAID 6, where parity calculations are required for each write operation. As the array grows, the system may experience slower write speeds due to the additional drives and increased parity operations. It is important to carefully monitor the performance of the RAID system after expansion to ensure that the array continues to meet the performance requirements of the organization. In some cases, it may be necessary to upgrade the RAID controller or optimize the configuration to maintain optimal performance.

RAID expansion can also be complicated by the limitations of the existing hardware. Many RAID controllers have specific limits on the number of drives they can support, and the controller may need to be upgraded or replaced to accommodate additional drives. Similarly, the physical space in the server or storage enclosure must be considered when expanding a RAID array. Ensuring that there is enough room for additional drives and that the cooling system can handle the increased heat output is essential for maintaining the reliability of the system. Expanding RAID arrays may also require careful planning to avoid downtime, as adding drives or changing configurations can potentially disrupt the system. To mitigate these challenges, it is advisable to plan the expansion carefully and ensure that all components, including the controller, enclosure, and cooling system, are capable of supporting the additional load.

Migration strategies are equally important for businesses looking to upgrade their RAID system or migrate to a different storage platform. RAID migration involves changing the RAID level or moving data from one array to another. This may be necessary when businesses need to improve performance, enhance redundancy, or optimize storage efficiency. For example, an organization using RAID 1 for mirroring may want to migrate to RAID 5 to take advantage of striping with parity, which offers more efficient use of storage while still providing fault tolerance. Similarly, a business using RAID 5 may decide to migrate to RAID 6 to provide an extra layer of redundancy with dual parity, protecting against the failure of two drives simultaneously.

The migration process can be complex and requires careful planning to ensure that data is not lost or corrupted during the transition. One of the primary concerns during RAID migration is the need to back up the data before making any changes. While most RAID controllers and software utilities offer the ability to perform non-disruptive migrations, there is always a risk that something could go wrong during the process. Therefore, it is essential to create a complete backup of all data before initiating the migration. This backup acts as a safety net in case the migration encounters any issues, such as hardware failures, corruption, or software incompatibilities.

Another consideration during RAID migration is the time and resources required to complete the process. Migrating from one RAID level to another can be time-consuming, especially if the array contains large amounts of data. During the migration process, the system may experience degraded performance, and in some cases, the array may need to be offline temporarily. Therefore, it is important to plan for potential downtime and ensure that business operations can continue without significant disruption. In enterprise environments, RAID migration may need to be coordinated with other IT activities, such as system maintenance or software upgrades, to minimize the impact on users and applications.

RAID migration also involves selecting the right RAID level to meet the new storage requirements. For instance, if an organization's data storage needs have increased, they may choose to migrate from a less fault-tolerant RAID level like RAID 1 to a more efficient and scalable solution such as RAID 5 or RAID 6. The decision should be based on the organization's priorities, such as performance, redundancy, or cost. RAID 5 offers a good balance between storage efficiency and fault tolerance, making it an attractive choice for many businesses. RAID 6 provides an additional layer of protection but at the cost of reduced storage efficiency and potentially slower write speeds due to dual parity. It is essential to assess the business's specific needs and choose a RAID level that provides the optimal balance of performance, redundancy, and cost.

In some cases, RAID migration may involve moving to a new storage platform altogether. As organizations scale, they may find that traditional on-premises RAID arrays no longer meet their needs, and they may decide to migrate to cloud-based storage or hybrid storage solutions that combine on-premises and cloud resources. Cloud storage offers benefits such as increased scalability, reduced upfront costs, and off-site data protection. However, migrating from a traditional RAID array to a cloud storage solution requires careful planning to ensure that data is transferred securely, efficiently, and with minimal downtime. Hybrid storage solutions, which combine local RAID arrays with cloud storage, offer the best of both worlds, providing high-speed access to local data while also leveraging the scalability and redundancy of cloud storage.

RAID expansion and migration are essential processes for ensuring that storage systems can grow and evolve with the needs of the organization. Whether expanding a RAID array to increase capacity or migrating to a new RAID level to enhance performance and redundancy, careful planning and execution are crucial to achieving a successful outcome. Both processes require consideration of the hardware, performance, and storage requirements, as well as the need for proper data backup and migration tools. When done correctly, RAID expansion and migration provide organizations with the ability to adapt to changing data storage needs while maintaining high levels of data integrity, performance, and availability.

The Impact of RAID on Storage Efficiency

RAID technology, or Redundant Array of Independent Disks, plays a significant role in the design and optimization of modern storage systems. The core objective of RAID is to combine multiple hard drives or solid-state drives into a single logical unit, which improves the overall performance, redundancy, and reliability of data storage. However, RAID also has a profound impact on storage efficiency, which is a critical consideration for businesses and organizations that deal with large volumes of data. Storage efficiency refers to the ratio of usable storage capacity to the total storage capacity of a system. It is a key metric when assessing the cost-effectiveness of a storage solution, as maximizing storage efficiency reduces the need for excessive hardware investments while maintaining the desired performance and fault tolerance.

The way in which RAID affects storage efficiency is largely dependent on the specific RAID level being used. Different RAID levels offer varying degrees of redundancy, performance, and capacity utilization. Some RAID configurations, such as RAID 0 and RAID 1, offer very different approaches to balancing storage capacity with data protection, while others, such as RAID 5 and RAID 6, attempt to strike a balance between redundancy, performance, and storage efficiency.

RAID 0, for instance, is known for its excellent storage efficiency, as it uses a method called striping to distribute data evenly across multiple disks. In a RAID 0 setup, there is no redundancy—data is split into blocks and written across two or more drives, resulting in a storage system that is as efficient as possible in terms of capacity. All of the storage space in a RAID 0 array is usable, and there is no overhead for redundancy. This makes RAID 0 ideal for applications that require high-speed access to data, such as video editing or gaming, where performance is the top priority. However, while RAID 0 offers optimal storage efficiency, it also comes with a significant tradeoff: it offers no fault tolerance. If one drive fails, all data is lost, making it unsuitable for systems where data protection is crucial.

In contrast, RAID 1, or mirroring, uses two drives to store identical copies of the data. While RAID 1 provides redundancy and fault tolerance, it comes at the cost of storage efficiency. Since each drive holds an exact copy of the data, only 50% of the total storage capacity is usable. For example, in a two-drive RAID 1 setup, if each drive has a capacity of 1 TB, only 1 TB of usable storage is available, even though the total capacity of the array is 2 TB. While RAID 1 offers excellent protection against data loss, its storage efficiency is lower compared to other RAID configurations that do not require mirroring. The main advantage of RAID 1 is its simplicity and its ability to provide a straightforward backup of data, but it is not an ideal choice for those who need to maximize storage capacity without sacrificing performance or redundancy.

RAID 5 and RAID 6 offer a more efficient solution in terms of storage utilization while still providing redundancy and fault tolerance. Both of these RAID levels use parity, which is a form of error-checking and recovery data, to protect the array against drive failures. In a RAID 5 array, data is striped across three or more drives, and a single parity block is distributed across the array. This means that if one drive fails, the data can be reconstructed from the remaining drives using the parity information. The storage efficiency of RAID 5 is better than RAID 1 because only one drive's worth of storage is used for parity, regardless of the number of drives in the array. For example, in a five-drive RAID 5 array, the usable capacity would be the total capacity of four drives, with one drive used for parity. This makes RAID 5 a popular choice for applications that require a good balance between redundancy, performance, and storage efficiency, such as file servers and storage systems in small to medium-sized businesses.

RAID 6 builds on the concept of RAID 5 by using two parity blocks instead of one, which allows it to tolerate the simultaneous failure of two drives without data loss. While RAID 6 provides more robust data protection than RAID 5, it does so at the cost of storage efficiency. In a RAID 6 array, two drives' worth of capacity is reserved for parity, meaning that only a portion of the total disk capacity is usable. For example, in a six-drive RAID 6 array, the usable storage would be the total capacity of four drives, with the other two drives used for parity. This makes RAID 6 a suitable choice for applications that require high levels of data protection, such as large-scale data centers or cloud storage, but it is less efficient in terms of storage utilization compared to RAID 5.

The impact of RAID on storage efficiency extends beyond the RAID level itself to the hardware and configuration choices made during setup. For instance, the size of the individual drives in a RAID array can affect how efficiently the storage system utilizes its capacity. When drives of different sizes are used in a RAID configuration, the smallest drive in the array typically determines the overall usable storage capacity. This can lead to wasted storage space if larger drives are used in an array where the smaller drives limit the overall capacity. To maximize storage efficiency, it is important to use drives of similar sizes and capacities, ensuring that all available storage is utilized effectively.

Another important factor in RAID and storage efficiency is the management of unused space, also known as free space or unallocated space. Some RAID configurations allow for the dynamic expansion of storage capacity as new drives are added to the array. While this feature can improve scalability and storage flexibility, it also requires careful management to ensure that unused space is effectively utilized. For instance, if an array is expanded with additional drives, the RAID controller or management software must ensure that the new drives are integrated into the array and that their storage space is properly allocated. Failure to manage this process can result in wasted space that reduces the overall efficiency of the system.

Storage efficiency in RAID arrays is also influenced by the performance demands of the applications using the array. For high-performance workloads, such as transactional databases or virtualized environments, the performance of the RAID system may be more important than storage efficiency. In such cases, RAID 0, which offers the best performance but no redundancy, may be used to optimize read and write speeds, while separate backup solutions are employed to protect the data. In contrast, environments that prioritize data protection, such as backup servers or archival systems, may prioritize RAID 1, RAID 5, or RAID 6 to ensure that the data is mirrored or protected with parity, even at the expense of some storage efficiency.

The growing use of solid-state drives (SSDs) in RAID arrays has further impacted storage efficiency. SSDs offer faster read and write speeds compared to traditional hard drives, but they come with different considerations in terms of wear leveling and write endurance. In SSD-based RAID arrays, the focus may shift from purely maximizing storage efficiency to balancing performance with long-term drive health. The wear-leveling mechanisms in SSDs, which distribute write operations across the drive to prevent excessive wear on individual cells, can have an impact on the overall storage utilization. In these cases, the efficiency of SSD-based RAID systems is often determined by factors such as write amplification and the lifespan of the drives, rather than by simple capacity calculation.

RAID technology plays a pivotal role in optimizing storage efficiency, but its effectiveness depends on the chosen RAID level, hardware configuration, and the specific needs of the system. By understanding how different RAID levels impact storage efficiency, businesses and organizations can make informed decisions that balance performance, redundancy, and capacity utilization. Whether for small-scale systems that prioritize cost-effectiveness or large-scale enterprise environments that demand high availability and fault tolerance, RAID provides a flexible and scalable solution for managing storage resources efficiently.

Fault Tolerance and RAID: How It Works

Fault tolerance is a fundamental concept in modern data storage systems, and RAID (Redundant Array of Independent Disks) has become one of the most widely adopted technologies for providing fault tolerance in computer systems. Fault tolerance refers to the ability of a system to continue operating properly in the event of a hardware failure, ensuring that data is still accessible and operations are not disrupted. RAID leverages multiple disk drives and different configurations to provide redundancy, meaning that if one or more drives fail, the system can still function without data loss or significant downtime. Understanding how RAID works to provide fault tolerance is essential for anyone involved in designing, configuring, or maintaining storage systems, especially in environments where data availability and reliability are critical.

At its core, RAID operates by combining multiple physical drives into a single logical unit, with the data being distributed across the drives in various ways, depending on the chosen RAID level. These levels differ in how they manage data redundancy, which directly impacts their ability to tolerate drive failures. RAID levels such as RAID 1, RAID 5, and RAID 6 are specifically designed with fault tolerance in mind, each using different methods to ensure that a system remains operational even if one or more drives experience failure.

RAID 1, often referred to as mirroring, is one of the simplest and most straightforward RAID configurations that provides fault tolerance. In a RAID 1 setup, data is duplicated exactly on two or more drives. If one drive fails, the system can continue to operate using the mirrored copy of the data on the other drive. RAID 1 offers excellent redundancy because each piece of data is stored on at least two drives, so even if one drive fails, there is always an identical copy of the data available on the other drive. This type of fault tolerance is particularly valuable in situations where data integrity is crucial and downtime needs to be minimized. The main drawback of RAID 1, however, is its storage inefficiency. Since data is mirrored, the total usable storage is halved. For instance, in a two-drive RAID 1 array, the usable storage capacity is equal to the capacity of one drive, as both drives contain identical copies of the data.

RAID 5 and RAID 6 take a different approach to fault tolerance by using parity data. These RAID levels distribute data and parity across multiple drives, allowing for more efficient use of storage while still providing redundancy. Parity is a form of error detection and correction data that is generated from the data being stored on the array. In the event of a drive failure, the lost data can be reconstructed by using the parity information stored on the remaining drives. RAID 5 uses a single parity block, meaning that it can tolerate the failure of one drive without losing data. When a drive fails in a RAID 5 array, the system will continue to operate in a degraded state, and the RAID controller will use the parity information to rebuild the data from the failed drive onto a replacement drive. RAID 6, on the other hand, uses two parity blocks, providing an extra layer of redundancy. This allows RAID 6 to tolerate the simultaneous failure of two drives, making it more fault-tolerant than RAID 5, but at the cost of increased storage overhead due to the additional parity data.

The fault tolerance in RAID systems is not limited to just drive failure; it also extends to how the system handles the degradation of the array during the rebuild process. When a drive fails in RAID 5 or RAID 6, the array enters a degraded mode, meaning that the system is still operational, but it is at risk. The remaining drives in the array handle both the normal I/O operations and the additional burden of rebuilding the lost data. During this rebuild process, performance may be slower than usual because the system is working harder to reconstruct the missing data. While RAID 5 can tolerate a single drive failure, if another drive fails during the rebuild, data loss will occur. RAID 6, with its dual parity, can handle two simultaneous drive failures, providing greater protection during the rebuild process. Despite the redundancy provided by RAID 6, the rebuild process still requires careful monitoring and management, as the system remains in a vulnerable state until the rebuild is complete.

One of the key features of RAID systems that contributes to their fault tolerance is their ability to automatically detect and recover from drive failures. In hardware-based RAID solutions, the RAID controller is responsible for monitoring the health of the drives in the array. When a failure occurs, the controller will automatically trigger the rebuild process and alert the system administrator. Many modern RAID controllers also support features such as hot spares, which are additional drives kept in standby mode. If a failure occurs, the hot spare can automatically replace the failed drive, and the rebuild process will begin without manual intervention. This ensures that the RAID array can continue to operate with minimal disruption while the failed drive is replaced.

Despite these robust fault tolerance capabilities, RAID systems are not immune to all types of failure. RAID is designed to protect against drive failures, but it does not protect against other forms of data loss, such as corruption, accidental deletion, or malware attacks. RAID will simply mirror or distribute the corrupted data across the array, making it impossible to recover the original, uncorrupted version of the data without a backup. This highlights the importance of combining RAID with other data protection strategies, such as regular backups, to ensure comprehensive protection against all types of data loss.

Additionally, while RAID provides fault tolerance for hardware failures, it cannot protect against failures of the RAID controller itself. If the RAID controller malfunctions or becomes damaged, the entire array can become inaccessible, and the data may be lost. To mitigate this risk, businesses often use redundant RAID controllers, which automatically take over if the primary controller fails. This ensures that the system remains operational even if the controller encounters an issue. Furthermore, regular maintenance and monitoring of the RAID system are crucial to identifying potential problems before they lead to failures.

RAID's fault tolerance mechanisms play a critical role in ensuring the reliability and availability of data in storage systems. By providing redundancy and enabling the system to continue operating despite drive failures, RAID helps prevent data loss and downtime, which are especially important in environments where data is mission-critical. RAID levels like RAID 1, RAID 5, and RAID 6 offer different trade-offs in terms of performance, capacity, and redundancy, but all contribute to improving fault tolerance and maintaining data accessibility. While RAID is not a complete solution for all data protection needs, it is an essential tool in a comprehensive data management strategy, offering businesses the ability to safeguard their data while ensuring continuous system uptime.

RAID Performance Optimization Techniques

RAID (Redundant Array of Independent Disks) technology is widely used to enhance both the performance and reliability of storage systems. By combining multiple physical drives into a single logical unit, RAID configurations improve access speeds, redundancy, and fault tolerance. However, the performance of a RAID array can be influenced by various factors, and optimizing these systems is critical for achieving the desired balance between speed, capacity, and redundancy. Implementing performance optimization techniques in RAID systems is essential to ensure that they meet the specific needs of businesses or environments with high data throughput requirements, such as databases, file servers, and virtualized systems.

One of the primary ways to optimize RAID performance is by selecting the right RAID level for the specific workload and performance goals. Different RAID levels offer varying benefits in terms of redundancy, storage efficiency, and performance. RAID 0, for example, focuses solely on performance by striping data across multiple drives, allowing for faster read and write speeds since data is written to multiple disks simultaneously. However, RAID 0 does not offer any fault tolerance, and the failure of one drive results in total data loss. RAID 10, a combination of RAID 1 and RAID 0, offers both improved performance and redundancy, providing faster data access through striping and data protection through mirroring. For environments where both speed and redundancy are crucial, RAID 10 is a common choice, offering a good balance between these competing needs.

RAID 5 and RAID 6 are also popular for performance optimization, especially in environments that require fault tolerance combined with reasonable performance. RAID 5 stripes data across multiple drives and uses parity to provide redundancy, while RAID 6 does the same but with an additional layer of parity for added fault tolerance. Both RAID 5 and RAID 6 distribute data and parity across the array, so read speeds are generally fast. However, write performance can be slower due to the need to calculate and write parity information. RAID 6, with its dual parity, may experience even more write latency compared to RAID 5. To optimize performance in these configurations, it is important to carefully monitor and manage the system's workload, ensuring that it is not overloaded with write-intensive tasks, which could degrade the overall performance of the array.

Another technique for improving RAID performance is to ensure that the system is using high-performance drives, particularly when working with demanding applications such as video editing, gaming, or large-scale database management. The speed of the drives within the RAID array directly impacts the performance of the entire system. For instance, using solid-state drives (SSDs) in a RAID array can significantly improve performance over traditional hard disk drives (HDDs), as SSDs have faster read and write speeds, lower latency, and better durability. Many businesses and data centers are now opting for SSD-based RAID arrays to meet the high-performance demands of modern workloads. The use of SSDs in RAID configurations such as RAID 10 or RAID 5 can dramatically increase throughput, reduce access times, and improve overall system responsiveness.

In addition to selecting the right RAID level and using high-performance drives, optimizing RAID controller performance is a key factor in maximizing system speed. The RAID controller is responsible for managing data distribution, parity calculations, and overall data integrity within the RAID array. RAID controllers often come with advanced features such as cache memory, battery-backed cache, and write acceleration capabilities, all of which can help improve performance. Cache memory, for instance, temporarily stores data before it is written to the drives, allowing for faster write operations by reducing the number of I/O operations needed. Battery-backed cache ensures that cached data is not lost in the event of a power failure, further enhancing system reliability.

To optimize the RAID controller's performance, businesses can implement settings that prioritize write operations or read operations depending on the workload. Some RAID controllers allow for the customization of the read/write cache policies, which can help accelerate specific types of data access. For instance, if a system is primarily handling read-heavy operations, enabling a read cache can improve performance by allowing the controller to fetch data more quickly from the cache rather than waiting for it to be retrieved from the drives. Similarly, for write-heavy systems, enabling write-back cache can improve write performance by allowing data to be temporarily stored in cache before being written to disk, which speeds up write operations.

Another aspect of RAID performance optimization is ensuring that the array is properly balanced and that the drives are optimally utilized. In large-scale RAID arrays, the performance can be negatively impacted if certain drives are overutilized while others are underutilized. This imbalance can occur when data is not evenly distributed across the drives, leading to bottlenecks where some drives handle a disproportionate amount of the I/O workload. To avoid this, administrators should regularly monitor the RAID array for performance anomalies and use RAID management tools to ensure that the data is evenly distributed across all drives. For example, most RAID management software provides diagnostics tools that can identify underperforming drives or an imbalanced workload, allowing administrators to address these issues before they impact system performance.

Another technique for optimizing RAID performance is through the use of disk alignment. In modern systems, especially those utilizing SSDs, proper disk alignment is essential for achieving optimal performance. Misaligned disk partitions can cause additional read/write operations and degrade performance, particularly in SSD-based RAID arrays. Disk alignment ensures that the partitions on the drives align properly with the underlying storage blocks, minimizing the number of unnecessary read/write cycles and improving the efficiency of the RAID array. This optimization is particularly important when migrating data from older storage systems to new RAID arrays, as misalignment can occur if the migration is not handled correctly.

Finally, optimizing the RAID configuration for specific applications can also significantly enhance performance. For instance, a RAID array designed for database operations may benefit from a different configuration than one designed for file storage or media production. For databases, optimizing the RAID array for random I/O performance may be crucial, as databases often require rapid access to small, random data blocks. In contrast, applications like video editing or large file transfers may benefit from sequential read/write operations, which can be enhanced by a RAID 0 configuration that focuses solely on striping data across multiple drives. Understanding the specific needs of the application or workload is key to selecting the optimal RAID configuration and optimizing performance.

The impact of RAID performance optimization techniques is far-reaching, as they ensure that systems can handle increasing data demands without sacrificing speed or reliability. By choosing the appropriate RAID level, using high-performance drives such as SSDs, optimizing RAID controllers and cache memory, balancing drive usage, aligning disks properly, and tailoring configurations to specific applications, businesses can achieve both improved performance and data protection. With the rapid growth of data in modern environments, especially in fields such as cloud computing, virtualized environments, and big data analytics, RAID optimization has become more critical than ever in ensuring that systems remain fast, reliable, and scalable.

RAID and Data Recovery: Handling System Failures

RAID (Redundant Array of Independent Disks) technology has become a cornerstone of modern data storage systems, offering both performance and fault tolerance. However, no system is immune to failure, and even RAID arrays can experience issues that compromise data integrity. The primary strength of RAID lies in its ability to handle drive failures gracefully and provide mechanisms to recover lost data, ensuring minimal disruption to business operations. Understanding how RAID facilitates data recovery during system failures and the processes involved in restoring data is crucial for administrators and businesses that rely on these systems for data protection and high availability.

When a RAID array experiences a failure, it doesn't always result in catastrophic data loss. The redundancy provided by RAID configurations, such as RAID 1, RAID 5, or RAID 6, ensures that if a drive fails, the data can still be accessed from the remaining drives. The level of redundancy and fault tolerance offered by RAID depends on the RAID level being used. RAID 1, for example, mirrors data across two drives, so if one drive fails, the data remains intact on the other. RAID 5 uses parity to protect against the failure of one drive, and RAID 6 offers an even higher level of protection with dual parity, allowing it to withstand the failure of two drives without losing data.

The ability of RAID systems to handle drive failures is vital for data recovery, as it allows the array to continue operating in a degraded mode while the failed drive is replaced. In RAID 5, when a single drive fails, the system can still function, although it operates with reduced performance. The RAID controller will use the parity data stored across the other drives to reconstruct the missing data from the failed drive. Once the failed drive is replaced, the RAID system automatically rebuilds the data onto the new drive, restoring redundancy and returning the system to a fully operational state.

The rebuild process in RAID is an essential component of data recovery. After a failed drive is replaced, the RAID system reconstructs the lost data by reading the parity information from the remaining drives and recalculating the missing data. This process can be time-consuming, especially for large arrays with substantial amounts of data. During the rebuild, the system is in a vulnerable state, as it relies on the parity data to reconstruct the lost information. If another drive fails during the rebuild process, the data could be lost, particularly in RAID 5, which can only tolerate one drive failure at a time. RAID 6, however, provides a higher level of protection with its dual parity, allowing for two simultaneous drive failures without data loss, which makes it a more resilient option in scenarios where drive failures occur during the rebuild.

One of the challenges with RAID data recovery is ensuring that the replacement drive is fully compatible with the rest of the array. In most cases, the new drive must be of the same size or larger than the drive being replaced to maintain the integrity of the array. Using a smaller drive will prevent the RAID system from rebuilding the data, as there will not be enough space to store the reconstructed data. Additionally, it is important to verify that the replacement drive is functioning correctly before beginning the rebuild process, as a faulty replacement drive can complicate or even prevent the rebuild from completing successfully.

In RAID configurations with multiple drives, such as RAID 5 and RAID 6, the process of handling system failures and recovering data can become more complex. If multiple drives fail simultaneously, especially in RAID 5, the system may no longer have enough redundancy to reconstruct the lost data. In such cases, RAID data recovery becomes much more difficult. However, specialized recovery software or services can be used to attempt data restoration, even in the event of multiple drive failures. These services often employ advanced techniques to recover data from damaged or degraded RAID arrays, although the success of such recovery is not always guaranteed. In high-stakes environments where data loss is unacceptable, having a backup strategy in place is essential to mitigate the risks associated with RAID failures.

It is crucial for businesses to implement a comprehensive backup strategy to complement the fault tolerance provided by RAID. RAID is designed to protect against hardware failures, but it cannot guard against data corruption, accidental deletion, or malicious attacks like ransomware. In the event of data corruption, the RAID array will mirror or distribute the corrupted data across the array, making it impossible to recover the original, uncorrupted version of the data. A regular backup schedule, whether performed on-site or off-site, ensures that there is always a copy of the data that can be restored if the RAID array experiences issues beyond simple drive failures.

A critical aspect of RAID and data recovery is the ongoing monitoring of the system's health. Most modern RAID controllers come with management software that allows administrators to monitor the status of the drives, alerting them to potential failures before they occur. Proactively replacing aging or failing drives can significantly reduce the likelihood of catastrophic data loss. Additionally, regular system checks and diagnostics can help identify potential issues, such as degraded performance or slow rebuild times, which may indicate underlying problems with the array.

In the case of a RAID failure, administrators should act quickly to mitigate the risk of data loss. The first step is to identify the failed drive and assess the health of the other drives in the array. If only one drive has failed in a RAID 5 array, the system can continue to operate in a degraded mode while the failed drive is replaced. During this time, the administrator should begin the rebuild process as soon as a compatible replacement drive is available. For RAID 6, the process is similar, but with the added benefit of tolerating two drive failures without immediate data loss. In both cases, it is essential to monitor the rebuild process closely to ensure that the system is functioning correctly and that no additional issues arise.

If multiple drives fail or if the rebuild process encounters errors, it may be necessary to seek professional data recovery services. These services use specialized tools to attempt data recovery from damaged or degraded RAID arrays, although recovery is not always possible, especially if multiple drives fail beyond the fault tolerance of the array. In extreme cases, where the data is critical, businesses may need to engage professional RAID recovery services that can handle complex data loss scenarios, although the cost of such services can be significant.

RAID systems provide an important layer of protection against data loss due to hardware failure, and the fault tolerance they offer is a critical aspect of modern storage infrastructures. While RAID can handle many types of failures and ensure the continued availability of data, it is not a catch-all solution for every type of data loss. For businesses relying on RAID for data protection, implementing a robust backup strategy, proactive system monitoring, and a well-defined data recovery plan are essential for ensuring that data remains secure and accessible, even in the event of system failures. With proper maintenance and planning, RAID systems can provide reliable and efficient data recovery, ensuring minimal downtime and data integrity in the face of unexpected failures.

The Role of RAID in Cloud Storage Architectures

Cloud storage has revolutionized the way organizations and individuals manage, store, and access data. It offers scalability, accessibility, and cost efficiency that on-premises storage solutions struggle to match. While cloud storage abstracts much of the complexity of physical infrastructure from end-users, the underlying architecture still relies on fundamental technologies like RAID (Redundant Array of Independent Disks) to ensure data redundancy, availability, and fault tolerance. The role of RAID in cloud storage architectures is significant because it provides a foundation for the reliability and performance of cloud-based data storage systems, which are essential for handling the vast amounts of data that modern applications and services generate.

RAID is a data storage virtualization technology that combines multiple physical disk drives into a single logical unit. The goal of RAID is to improve performance, increase data availability, and protect data by offering redundancy. Different RAID levels achieve these objectives in varying ways, depending on the configuration. For example, RAID 1 (mirroring) creates an exact copy of data across two or more drives, while RAID 5 (striping with parity) distributes data and parity across multiple drives, allowing for fault tolerance with less storage overhead. RAID 6 is similar to RAID 5 but offers even greater fault tolerance by using double parity. These RAID levels are often employed in cloud storage architectures to ensure that data is available even in the event of hardware failure, which is critical for maintaining the reliability of cloud-based services.

In the context of cloud storage, RAID plays a crucial role in providing the fault tolerance required to ensure data integrity and availability. Cloud service providers typically use a large number of storage nodes to manage their data storage infrastructure. These nodes are physical servers equipped with multiple hard drives or solid-state drives (SSDs) that are organized into RAID configurations. By using RAID, cloud providers can ensure that if one of the drives within a node fails, the data remains accessible because the redundant information is stored on other drives within the same array. RAID also allows for quick recovery from hardware failures, reducing the downtime experienced by customers accessing cloud storage.

In large-scale cloud storage environments, the use of RAID allows providers to manage petabytes of data across thousands of drives while maintaining high levels of performance and redundancy. For example, in a typical public cloud deployment, cloud service providers might use RAID 5 or RAID 6 configurations within each storage node to strike a balance between fault tolerance, storage efficiency, and performance. RAID 5, in particular, is popular in cloud environments because it provides fault tolerance without wasting a significant amount of storage space. However, as the size of the data grows, cloud providers often have to consider factors such as data throughput, drive performance, and network latency to ensure that RAID configurations remain effective.

RAID configurations in cloud storage architectures are often coupled with other advanced technologies to further enhance data protection and accessibility. For instance, cloud providers may combine RAID with data replication across geographically dispersed data centers to provide even greater redundancy. In this setup, copies of data stored in a RAID array are replicated across multiple locations, ensuring that even if an entire data center were to experience an outage, the data would still be available from other locations. This type of multi-site redundancy is essential for maintaining high availability in cloud storage systems, particularly for businesses and applications that require continuous access to their data.

In addition to improving data redundancy and availability, RAID can also play a role in optimizing the performance of cloud storage systems. For cloud providers that handle large-scale data operations, performance is a critical factor, and RAID helps enhance system throughput by distributing data across multiple drives. For example, RAID 0, which uses striping to distribute data evenly across multiple disks, can be used in cloud storage environments where high-performance read and write operations are required. While RAID 0 offers no redundancy and carries the risk of data loss in the event of a drive failure, it can be useful in specific scenarios where performance is prioritized over fault tolerance. However, in production environments, the use of RAID 1, RAID 5, or RAID 6 is more common, as they combine performance benefits with the additional security of redundancy.

RAID also influences the scalability of cloud storage systems. As the amount of data stored in the cloud grows, the storage infrastructure needs to be able to expand efficiently. RAID enables this by allowing cloud providers to add additional storage nodes to the array without significant disruption to the overall system. New drives can be integrated into existing RAID arrays, and the storage capacity can be increased incrementally. This scalability is particularly important in cloud storage architectures that serve large, dynamic user bases with fluctuating storage needs. The ability to seamlessly scale storage resources while maintaining data availability is a key benefit of using RAID in cloud environments.

Another important consideration when using RAID in cloud storage is the type of drives employed. Traditionally, RAID was designed for use with hard disk drives (HDDs), but with the advent of solid-state drives (SSDs), cloud providers are increasingly adopting SSD-based RAID configurations. SSDs offer faster read and write speeds, lower latency, and higher durability compared to traditional HDDs, which can significantly improve the overall performance of a cloud storage system. RAID configurations, such as RAID 10 or RAID 5, can be implemented using SSDs to deliver high-speed access to cloud data, which is especially beneficial for applications that require rapid data processing or low-latency access. Additionally, as SSD prices continue to drop, the use of SSDs in RAID arrays within cloud storage systems becomes increasingly cost-effective, allowing providers to deliver both high performance and reliable redundancy at scale.

Despite the many advantages of RAID in cloud storage architectures, there are also challenges and limitations to consider. One of the primary concerns is the performance penalty associated with parity-based RAID levels, such as RAID 5 and RAID 6. While these configurations offer fault tolerance, they require extra processing power to calculate parity data during write operations, which can slow down write speeds. In cloud storage environments, where high throughput is often necessary, this performance hit can be significant, particularly when large volumes of data are being written simultaneously. To mitigate this, cloud providers may use hardware-accelerated RAID controllers or offload parity calculations to dedicated processors, but these solutions can increase the complexity and cost of the system.

Another challenge is the management and monitoring of RAID arrays at scale. As cloud storage systems grow, so too does the complexity of managing multiple RAID configurations across numerous storage nodes. Cloud providers must have robust monitoring tools in place to track the health of individual drives, ensure that rebuilds occur smoothly after a failure, and manage the balancing of workloads across RAID arrays. Additionally, data migration between RAID configurations or storage tiers can be challenging, especially in dynamic cloud environments where resources are constantly changing.

RAID plays an integral role in the architecture of cloud storage systems, offering crucial benefits in terms of redundancy, performance, and scalability. It ensures that cloud storage remains highly available and reliable, even in the face of drive failures or other hardware issues. Through a combination of RAID configurations, data replication, and advanced storage management techniques, cloud providers can meet the growing demands for data storage while maintaining high levels of performance and data integrity. As cloud environments continue to evolve and handle larger and more diverse data workloads, the role of RAID in optimizing and securing cloud storage will remain essential.

RAID in High-Performance Computing Environments

High-performance computing (HPC) environments are designed to handle intensive computational tasks, such as scientific simulations, data analysis, machine learning, and large-scale modeling. These environments rely on sophisticated hardware and storage systems to deliver the speed, efficiency, and reliability required to support demanding applications. RAID (Redundant Array of Independent Disks) plays a crucial role in HPC environments by providing fault tolerance, enhancing storage performance, and ensuring data availability, which are critical for the smooth operation of high-performance systems. The use of RAID in HPC is indispensable for achieving the required throughput and minimizing downtime, as well as for maintaining the integrity of large datasets used in computational research and analysis.

In an HPC environment, storage systems must handle vast amounts of data with low latency and high throughput. These environments often generate and process data in real time, and delays in accessing this data can significantly affect the performance of simulations, data analysis, and other computational tasks. RAID addresses this challenge by improving the speed of read and write operations through data striping and caching. For example, in RAID 0, data is striped across multiple disks, allowing for parallel access to the data, which significantly increases throughput. RAID 0 is ideal in scenarios where speed is the primary concern and where data redundancy is not a requirement. However, RAID 0 comes with the risk of data loss in the event of a drive failure, as there is no redundancy built into the array.

RAID 10, a combination of RAID 1 (mirroring) and RAID 0 (striping), is often preferred in high-performance computing environments that require both speed and redundancy. In RAID 10, data is mirrored across pairs of drives for redundancy, and the mirrored drives are then striped for performance. This configuration provides fault tolerance, as the system can continue operating even if one drive in a mirrored pair fails, and it also delivers improved performance by allowing for parallel read and write operations. RAID 10 is particularly useful in HPC environments where the system cannot afford significant downtime, such as in scientific research, financial modeling, and other data-intensive tasks that require both high performance and data protection.

RAID 5 and RAID 6 are also commonly used in HPC environments, especially in situations where storage efficiency is a key consideration. These RAID levels use parity to provide redundancy while minimizing the overhead associated with full data duplication. In RAID 5, data is striped across multiple drives, and parity information is distributed across the array. If a drive fails, the data can be reconstructed using the parity information from the remaining drives. RAID 6 is similar to RAID 5 but uses two sets of parity data, which allows it to tolerate the simultaneous failure of two drives. While RAID 5 and RAID 6 provide fault tolerance with less storage overhead than RAID 1, they may experience slower write speeds due to the need to calculate and update the parity data during write operations. In HPC environments, where read-heavy tasks are common, RAID 5 and RAID 6 can provide a good balance of redundancy, performance, and storage efficiency.

Despite the many advantages of RAID, there are certain challenges when using RAID in high-performance computing environments. One of the primary challenges is ensuring that the RAID array can handle the massive amounts of data generated by HPC workloads without creating bottlenecks in data access. In HPC systems, where large datasets are processed simultaneously, the speed at which data can be read from or written to the storage system is critical. Even small delays in data retrieval can lead to significant slowdowns in computation, which can compromise the overall performance of the system. Optimizing RAID configurations to meet these demands often involves balancing the choice of RAID level, the type of drives used, and the capabilities of the RAID controller.

In high-performance environments, the type of storage devices used in the RAID array can also impact performance. Traditional hard disk drives (HDDs) are often slower and may not be able to meet the high throughput demands of HPC applications. Solid-state drives (SSDs), on the other hand, offer significantly faster read and write speeds and lower latency compared to HDDs, making them ideal for use in RAID configurations for HPC environments. SSD-based RAID arrays can greatly enhance the overall performance of HPC systems by providing faster access to data and reducing the time needed to complete computational tasks. As SSD prices continue to decrease, SSD-based RAID arrays are becoming increasingly popular in high-performance storage solutions, offering both high speed and reliability for data-intensive applications.

Another consideration in RAID-based HPC environments is the role of RAID controllers. The RAID controller is responsible for managing the distribution of data across the drives, handling parity calculations, and managing the overall health of the RAID array. In high-performance environments, the choice of RAID controller can significantly impact system performance. Hardware RAID controllers, which have dedicated processors and memory, can offload RAID operations from the host CPU, allowing the system to focus on computational tasks rather than storage management. These controllers often come with features such as cache memory, which can further improve the performance of the RAID array by temporarily storing data before it is written to disk. Additionally, RAID controllers with battery-backed cache provide greater reliability by ensuring that data is not lost in the event of a power failure.

The scalability of RAID configurations is another important factor to consider in high-performance computing environments. As the storage requirements of HPC systems grow, it is essential to have a RAID setup that can scale to accommodate increasing amounts of data. RAID systems can be expanded by adding additional drives to the array, allowing for increased capacity without significant disruption to the system. This scalability is particularly useful in HPC environments where the data storage needs are constantly evolving, and the system must be able to grow along with the demands of the application. Cloud-based RAID solutions are also becoming increasingly popular in HPC, as they provide virtually unlimited storage scalability, allowing users to dynamically increase storage capacity as needed.

In addition to providing fault tolerance, redundancy, and performance optimization, RAID also helps protect data in high-performance computing environments by enabling faster data recovery after a failure. In the event of a drive failure, the RAID array can continue to operate in a degraded state, ensuring that the system remains functional while the failed drive is replaced. Once the failed drive is replaced, the RAID system will automatically rebuild the data onto the new drive, restoring the array to its full capacity. This capability is particularly important in HPC environments, where downtime is costly, and quick data recovery is essential to minimize disruptions in computational tasks.

RAID plays a vital role in ensuring the reliability, performance, and scalability of high-performance computing systems. Whether through the use of RAID 10 for both redundancy and performance or RAID 5 and RAID 6 for efficient storage with fault tolerance, RAID technologies are essential for meeting the demanding requirements of modern HPC workloads. With the right combination of RAID configuration, storage devices, and RAID controllers, high-performance computing environments can deliver the speed, reliability, and scalability needed for complex data processing tasks.

Understanding RAID in Network-Attached Storage (NAS)

Network-attached storage (NAS) has become a fundamental component in modern IT infrastructure, providing a centralized solution for data storage, access, and management. A NAS system allows multiple users and devices to access files over a network, making it ideal for collaborative environments, backup solutions, and data archiving. One of the core technologies that underpin NAS systems is RAID, or Redundant Array of Independent Disks. RAID enables NAS devices to offer increased data redundancy, fault tolerance, and performance by utilizing multiple hard drives or solid-state drives. Understanding the role of RAID in NAS systems is essential for ensuring that the storage solution is both reliable and efficient, capable of meeting the demands of businesses and users who rely on quick, uninterrupted access to their data.

RAID in a NAS environment functions by combining multiple physical storage devices into a single logical unit. This setup improves performance and ensures that data is protected in case of hardware failure. Depending on the RAID level used, NAS systems can offer varying degrees of redundancy, storage efficiency, and performance enhancements. The choice of RAID level in a NAS system is largely driven by the balance between these factors. For example, RAID 0 is often used when performance is the priority, as it stripes data across two or more drives, allowing for faster read and write operations. However, RAID 0 provides no redundancy, meaning that if one drive fails, all data on the array is lost.

RAID 1, on the other hand, is commonly used in NAS systems that require redundancy. In RAID 1, data is mirrored across two drives, meaning that an exact copy of the data is stored on both drives. If one drive fails, the other drive continues to hold an intact copy of the data, ensuring that it remains accessible. RAID 1 is popular in small NAS devices and environments where data protection is more important than storage capacity, as it effectively halves the total usable storage capacity. While it provides excellent data redundancy, RAID 1 sacrifices storage efficiency, making it less suitable for environments that require large amounts of storage.

RAID 5 and RAID 6 are among the most commonly used RAID levels in NAS systems, particularly in larger, more enterprise-grade environments. RAID 5 offers a good balance between fault tolerance, performance, and storage efficiency by striping data across multiple drives and distributing parity information across the array. Parity is a form of error-correction data that allows the system to reconstruct lost data in the event of a single drive failure. RAID 5 can tolerate the failure of one drive without data loss, making it an attractive choice for NAS systems that require both reliability and storage efficiency. However, RAID 5 does have a performance overhead associated with parity calculations, which can affect write speeds, especially in write-heavy environments.

RAID 6 is similar to RAID 5 but provides an additional layer of redundancy by using two sets of parity data instead of one. This allows RAID 6 to tolerate the simultaneous failure of two drives without data loss, providing even greater fault tolerance than RAID 5. However, the added redundancy comes at the cost of additional storage overhead, as two drives' worth of capacity is used for parity rather than data. RAID 6 is often used in environments where high data availability is critical, such as in larger NAS systems used for data archiving, backup, or large-scale file storage.

In NAS systems, RAID not only provides fault tolerance but also enhances performance. For instance, in configurations such as RAID 10, which combines RAID 1 and RAID 0, data is both mirrored and striped, offering both redundancy and increased performance. RAID 10 is often used in NAS environments that require high throughput, such as video editing or media streaming, where fast read and write speeds are essential. By striping data across multiple disks, RAID 10 improves I/O performance, while the mirroring of data ensures that the system remains operational even if a drive fails.

The integration of RAID into NAS systems also enhances data management and scalability. As businesses grow, their data storage needs typically expand, and RAID provides a flexible way to scale storage capacity. Most modern NAS systems are designed to support RAID expansion, allowing users to add additional drives or replace smaller drives with larger ones without significant disruptions. This scalability is especially beneficial in NAS systems used by businesses with evolving storage requirements, such as growing databases, large multimedia files, or backups.

Additionally, RAID can be combined with other technologies to further optimize NAS performance and redundancy. For example, many NAS systems implement features such as caching and tiered storage, which work alongside RAID to enhance performance. Caching involves temporarily storing frequently accessed data in faster storage, such as SSDs, to reduce latency and improve access speeds. Tiered storage, on the other hand, involves automatically moving less frequently accessed data to slower storage tiers, such as HDDs, while keeping active data on faster drives. These features, when combined with RAID, ensure that NAS systems can handle both high-speed access and large amounts of data without compromising performance or redundancy.

While RAID provides significant benefits in terms of data protection and performance, it is not without its challenges. One of the primary considerations when using RAID in NAS systems is the risk of data loss during the rebuild process. When a drive fails in a RAID 5 or RAID 6 array, the array enters a degraded state, and the remaining drives are responsible for both data access and parity calculations. During this time, the system is vulnerable to further failures, and if another drive fails before the rebuild process is completed, data loss may occur. This highlights the importance of regular monitoring and proactive maintenance to detect failing drives before they cause significant problems.

Furthermore, RAID configurations, particularly those with parity, can have an impact on write performance. The process of calculating and updating parity data during write operations introduces a performance overhead, which may be noticeable in high-demand environments. To mitigate this, NAS systems may use dedicated hardware RAID controllers or caching techniques to offload some of the processing work from the system's CPU. Using solid-state drives (SSDs) in conjunction with RAID can also help improve performance, especially in write-heavy workloads, as SSDs offer faster data access speeds than traditional hard disk drives.

Another challenge in NAS systems using RAID is the need for backup and disaster recovery strategies. While RAID provides fault tolerance and redundancy within the storage system itself, it does not protect against other forms of data loss, such as accidental deletion, corruption, or ransomware attacks. For comprehensive data protection, NAS systems must be complemented by regular backups to offsite storage or cloud-based solutions. This ensures that even if the RAID array fails or data becomes corrupted, a reliable backup is available for restoration.

RAID plays a pivotal role in ensuring the reliability, performance, and scalability of NAS systems, which are critical for data storage in modern IT environments. By providing redundancy, fault tolerance, and performance optimization, RAID enables NAS devices to meet the growing data storage demands of businesses and users. From simple home storage solutions to large enterprise-level data centers, RAID provides the backbone for ensuring data integrity, availability, and accessibility in a wide range of NAS applications. As technology continues to evolve and data storage needs become more complex, the role of RAID in NAS systems will remain a vital aspect of managing data in an increasingly interconnected and data-driven world.

RAID in Storage Area Networks (SAN)

Storage Area Networks (SANs) are highly specialized, high-performance networks designed to provide access to consolidated, block-level data storage. SANs are used extensively in enterprise environments where large amounts of data need to be stored, managed, and accessed quickly and reliably. The storage within a SAN is typically made up of several physical storage devices that are connected through a dedicated network. RAID (Redundant Array of Independent Disks) technology plays a significant role in the design and functionality of SANs by providing the necessary redundancy, performance optimization, and fault tolerance needed to ensure high availability and data protection. In SANs, RAID is employed to enhance the overall performance and reliability of storage systems by protecting against disk failures and improving throughput, especially in environments that demand continuous access to critical data.

In a typical SAN configuration, storage devices such as hard drives or solid-state drives are connected to a network, and data can be accessed from servers or other devices on the same network. SANs use protocols like Fibre Channel, iSCSI, or FCoE (Fibre Channel over Ethernet) to facilitate communication between the storage arrays and the servers. These protocols allow SANs to deliver high-speed data transfers, making them ideal for use in environments where large volumes of data need to be processed or where fast data access is essential, such as in database management, data centers, and virtualized environments. RAID technology is used in SANs to help mitigate the risk of data loss, increase data access speeds, and optimize the performance of the storage array.

One of the primary reasons RAID is used in SAN environments is to provide fault tolerance and redundancy. In a typical SAN, where large amounts of data are stored across multiple disks, the potential for drive failure is ever-present. Without redundancy, a single disk failure could result in the loss of critical data, leading to service interruptions or even system outages. RAID addresses this risk by using different configurations that ensure data is mirrored, striped, or protected by parity, depending on the RAID level chosen. For example, RAID 1 mirrors data across two or more drives, ensuring that an identical copy of the data is available if one drive fails. RAID 5, which uses a combination of data striping and parity, can tolerate a single drive failure while still maintaining data integrity, making it an attractive choice for SANs that require both redundancy and storage efficiency.

RAID 6 takes this redundancy a step further by providing double parity, allowing it to tolerate the failure of two drives simultaneously. This makes RAID 6 particularly valuable in large-scale SAN environments, where the likelihood of multiple drive failures may be higher due to the sheer number of drives in use. Both RAID 5 and RAID 6 provide excellent fault tolerance without sacrificing too much usable storage capacity, as the parity data required for reconstruction is distributed across the drives, rather than duplicating the data on each drive. These configurations are commonly employed in SANs where high availability and disaster recovery are critical.

In addition to providing fault tolerance, RAID also plays a key role in enhancing the performance of SANs. RAID 0, which stripes data across multiple drives without redundancy, offers the highest performance by allowing simultaneous access to different parts of the data. While RAID 0 is not typically used in production SANs due to the lack of redundancy, it can be useful in environments where performance is prioritized over data protection, such as in temporary or non-critical storage applications. In contrast, RAID 10, which combines the performance benefits of RAID 0 with the redundancy of RAID 1, is often used in SANs that require high throughput, low latency, and data redundancy. RAID 10 delivers superior read and write performance compared to other RAID levels while still maintaining fault tolerance, making it ideal for applications that demand both speed and reliability.

In a SAN, the use of RAID can also help optimize storage efficiency. As businesses and data centers continue to scale their storage needs, the ability to effectively manage large volumes of data becomes increasingly important. RAID allows SAN administrators to maximize storage capacity while maintaining data protection. For example, RAID 5 and RAID 6 enable organizations to store more data per disk while still providing redundancy and fault tolerance. This storage efficiency can be crucial in high-demand environments where data must be stored cost-effectively without compromising performance or availability.

Moreover, RAID in SANs is essential for managing the growth of data in a scalable manner. As the need for storage increases, adding additional disks to a RAID array allows the SAN to scale its capacity without interrupting the entire system. With RAID, administrators can expand storage arrays by adding new drives or replacing existing drives with larger ones, enabling the SAN to grow as the business's storage requirements expand. This scalability ensures that SANs can keep pace with the demands of large-scale data management and provides the flexibility to accommodate changing workloads, whether in virtualized environments, cloud applications, or big data analytics.

While RAID offers several benefits in SAN environments, there are challenges that must be addressed when configuring RAID in large-scale storage systems. One of the primary challenges is the performance overhead associated with certain RAID levels, especially when dealing with write-intensive applications. For example, in RAID 5 and RAID 6, the parity calculations required for write operations can introduce latency and reduce write performance. In SAN environments where high write throughput is necessary, this performance penalty may be noticeable. To mitigate these issues, many organizations opt for using hardware RAID controllers with dedicated processors and cache memory, which can offload some of the parity calculations from the main system and improve overall performance. Additionally, using SSDs (Solid State Drives) in RAID arrays can significantly enhance performance by providing faster data access speeds and lower latency compared to traditional hard drives.

Another challenge in implementing RAID in SANs is managing the rebuild process after a drive failure. When a drive fails in a RAID array, the system enters a degraded mode, and the remaining drives handle both regular data access and the process of rebuilding the lost data. This rebuild process can place additional strain on the system, particularly in large-scale SANs with large amounts of data. It is essential to closely monitor the rebuild process and ensure that it completes successfully to avoid further disruptions or the risk of data loss in case another drive fails during the rebuild. Many modern SANs have built-in tools and monitoring features that can help administrators track the status of the RAID array and take appropriate action to resolve any issues before they affect the system.

RAID plays an integral role in the design and operation of Storage Area Networks, offering both performance optimization and fault tolerance that are critical for maintaining the integrity and availability of data in large-scale environments. Whether used in conjunction with hard drives or SSDs, RAID technology ensures that data can be accessed quickly, efficiently, and securely, even in the event of hardware failure. As organizations continue to rely on SANs to handle increasingly complex and voluminous data, RAID remains a key technology for ensuring that these storage systems can meet the performance and reliability demands of modern IT infrastructures.

The Future of RAID: Emerging Technologies

As data storage needs continue to evolve in the face of growing digital content, high-performance applications, and an expanding internet of things (IoT), the traditional methods of managing and securing data are being scrutinized and upgraded. RAID (Redundant Array of Independent Disks) technology, which has been a cornerstone of data redundancy and performance optimization for decades, is undergoing significant changes as emerging technologies reshape the landscape of data storage. While RAID continues to be an essential tool for ensuring data availability and fault tolerance, the advent of new hardware, software, and storage paradigms is influencing how RAID is used in modern IT infrastructures. These innovations, driven by advancements in storage media, cloud computing, and artificial intelligence, promise to redefine the role of RAID in both enterprise and consumer environments.

One of the most significant developments that will impact the future of RAID is the widespread adoption of solid-state drives (SSDs) as a primary storage medium. SSDs offer several advantages over traditional hard disk drives (HDDs), including faster data access speeds, lower latency, and greater durability. The transition from HDDs to SSDs in RAID configurations presents new opportunities for performance optimization. RAID arrays that leverage SSDs can deliver dramatically faster read and write speeds, which are crucial for high-performance computing applications, large databases, and real-time analytics. SSDs can reduce the performance bottlenecks that have traditionally been associated with RAID, particularly in configurations that require high-throughput data operations.

However, SSDs also introduce new challenges to RAID configurations. One of the most notable issues is the limited lifespan of SSDs compared to HDDs. SSDs wear out over time due to the finite number of write cycles they can handle, which could potentially compromise the redundancy and fault tolerance offered by RAID. RAID levels like RAID 5 and RAID 6, which rely on parity to reconstruct lost data, may experience slower rebuild times when SSDs are used, as the wear leveling inherent to SSD technology can result in uneven write operations. As a result, RAID configurations in SSD-based storage systems must evolve to address the unique characteristics of solid-state technology, ensuring that these systems can continue to offer both speed and reliability in high-demand environments.

In addition to the adoption of SSDs, the growing prominence of NVMe (Non-Volatile Memory Express) drives is poised to reshape RAID technology. NVMe drives provide a faster, more efficient interface for accessing NAND flash memory compared to traditional SATA and SAS interfaces. NVMe offers higher data transfer rates and lower latency, making it ideal for applications that require rapid data processing, such as machine learning, artificial intelligence, and data-intensive workloads. As NVMe technology continues to mature, it is likely that RAID systems will need to adapt to take full advantage of these advancements in speed and throughput. New RAID levels and controller architectures designed specifically for NVMe drives will enable even faster data access, ensuring that RAID continues to meet the performance demands of modern storage environments.

Another emerging technology that will influence the future of RAID is software-defined storage (SDS). SDS abstracts the management of storage resources from the underlying hardware, allowing administrators to manage storage more dynamically and flexibly. By decoupling storage software from physical devices, SDS enables organizations to implement more agile and scalable storage solutions. In the context of RAID, SDS can facilitate the creation of virtual RAID arrays that span multiple storage devices, including SSDs, HDDs, and even cloud-based storage. This flexibility allows RAID to be used more efficiently in hybrid and multi-cloud environments, where different storage tiers are utilized based on performance and cost requirements.

SDS also integrates well with other emerging technologies, such as artificial intelligence (AI) and machine learning, which are increasingly being used to optimize storage management. AI-driven algorithms can analyze data access patterns, predict drive failures, and optimize RAID configurations in real time, automatically adjusting the array for maximum performance and redundancy. This level of automation reduces the need for manual intervention and can help prevent data loss by proactively addressing potential issues before they become critical. As AI continues to be integrated into RAID and storage management systems, the future of RAID will likely include more intelligent, self-healing systems that can adapt to changing workloads and hardware failures.

The rise of cloud storage and hybrid cloud environments also has a significant impact on the future of RAID. While traditional RAID configurations have typically been used in on-premises storage systems, cloud-based storage solutions are increasingly incorporating RAID-like redundancy and fault tolerance features to protect data in the cloud. Cloud storage providers often use a combination of data replication, erasure coding, and RAID techniques to ensure that data is distributed across multiple locations and remains available even in the event of server or disk failures. RAID is being integrated with cloud-native technologies to offer the same high levels of redundancy and performance that on-premises storage systems have historically provided. As cloud adoption grows, the lines between traditional RAID and cloud-based redundancy models will continue to blur, leading to more hybrid storage architectures that combine the best of both worlds.

As RAID evolves in response to these emerging technologies, one area of focus is the need for enhanced scalability. Traditional RAID systems were designed to be relatively static in terms of storage capacity. Expanding a RAID array typically involved replacing drives with larger ones or adding more drives, which could be a time-consuming process. However, as data storage demands continue to grow exponentially, RAID must adapt to more dynamic environments where scaling up or down quickly is essential. Newer RAID solutions are being designed with scalability in mind, allowing organizations to expand storage capacity seamlessly without disrupting operations. This scalability will be particularly important in environments like big data analytics, where the volume of data being processed increases rapidly and where rapid expansion of storage resources is necessary to keep up with the pace of growth.

Another key area of innovation is the development of storage solutions that combine RAID with other data protection technologies, such as erasure coding. Erasure coding is a method of data protection that splits data into fragments, encodes it with redundant data, and distributes the fragments across multiple storage devices. This technology provides greater storage efficiency than traditional RAID while offering the same level of fault tolerance. In the future, RAID and erasure coding may be integrated to provide even more reliable and efficient data protection solutions, combining the best aspects of both technologies to meet the needs of modern storage environments.

The future of RAID is undoubtedly intertwined with the development of these emerging technologies, which are pushing the boundaries of what is possible in data storage. As RAID continues to evolve, it will remain a critical component in ensuring data availability, redundancy, and performance. With the increasing demands of modern applications, the next generation of RAID systems will need to be more flexible, intelligent, and scalable than ever before, capable of meeting the needs of high-performance computing, cloud environments, and data-intensive industries. Whether through the adoption of SSDs, NVMe drives, software-defined storage, or AI-driven optimizations, RAID will continue to be at the heart of data protection strategies, adapting to new technological advancements while maintaining its core role in the management of data integrity.

RAID and Data Security: Protecting Against Cyber Threats

In today's digital age, data security has become one of the most critical concerns for businesses and individuals alike. With the increasing frequency of cyberattacks, such as ransomware, data breaches, and malicious intrusions, ensuring the protection of sensitive data is paramount. RAID (Redundant Array of Independent Disks) plays a vital role in data security by providing redundancy, fault tolerance, and performance optimization to prevent data loss and ensure that data remains available in the event of hardware failure. However, while RAID provides essential protection against physical hardware failures, it is important to understand its limitations when it comes to protecting against cyber threats. As cyber threats continue to evolve in complexity, RAID technology, in conjunction with other security measures, must be an integral part of a multi-layered approach to data protection.

RAID primarily enhances data security by ensuring that data is not lost in the event of a drive failure. In configurations such as RAID 1 (mirroring), RAID 5 (striping with parity), and RAID 6 (dual parity), RAID creates redundant copies of data across multiple disks. This redundancy allows the system to continue functioning even when one or more drives fail, as the data can be reconstructed from the remaining drives. In RAID 1, for example, data is mirrored across two or more drives, and if one drive fails, the mirrored copy on the second drive is still available. Similarly, RAID 5 and RAID 6 provide fault tolerance using parity data, which can be used to reconstruct lost data if a drive fails. These features ensure that critical data remains accessible, reducing the risk of data loss due to hardware failure.

While RAID is effective at protecting against physical failures, it is not designed to defend against cyber threats such as hacking, malware, or ransomware. For instance, if an attacker gains access to a RAID array, they can potentially delete or corrupt data. Because RAID is focused on providing redundancy, it will simply mirror or distribute the corrupted data across the array, making it impossible to recover the original uncorrupted version of the data. In the case of ransomware, for example, if an infected file is stored on a RAID array, the malware can spread and encrypt the data on all drives within the array, effectively rendering it inaccessible. In such cases, RAID's redundancy does not help protect the data from corruption or encryption caused by malicious software.

To combat these cyber threats, RAID must be part of a broader security strategy that includes additional protective measures such as regular backups, encryption, access control, and advanced threat detection systems. Backups, for example, are essential for recovering from cyberattacks. Since RAID does not protect against the deletion, corruption, or encryption of data, having a reliable backup system is crucial. Regularly scheduled backups to an offsite location or cloud storage can ensure that, even in the event of a ransomware attack or data breach, a clean, uncorrupted copy of the data is available for restoration. These backups should be maintained on separate systems, isolated from the primary storage network, to minimize the risk of them being compromised in the same attack.

Encryption is another essential security measure that complements RAID in protecting data from unauthorized access. RAID ensures that data is available even in the event of hardware failure, but it does not protect the data from unauthorized access. Encryption helps secure sensitive information by making it unreadable to anyone without the correct decryption key. In a RAID system, encryption can be implemented at the disk level, where all data written to the storage drives is automatically encrypted. This ensures that even if an attacker physically gains access to the RAID array, they will not be able to read or manipulate the data without the decryption key. Encryption can also be applied to network traffic, protecting data in transit as it moves between servers and clients, further enhancing the overall security posture of the system.

Access control is another crucial layer of security that works alongside RAID to prevent unauthorized access to data. Limiting access to sensitive data ensures that only authorized users or systems can interact with the storage devices. This can be achieved through strong user authentication, multi-factor authentication (MFA), and role-based access control (RBAC) policies. By restricting access based on the principle of least privilege, organizations can minimize the risk of insider threats and external attacks. In a RAID environment, access control can be configured at the storage level, ensuring that only users with the appropriate permissions are able to access or modify the data stored on the array.

Advanced threat detection and monitoring systems are also vital for protecting against cyber threats in RAID-based storage systems. These systems can detect abnormal behavior, unauthorized access attempts, or signs of a cyberattack, allowing administrators to take action before the attack escalates. For example, monitoring tools can track login attempts, file modifications, and system performance, alerting administrators if there are signs of malicious activity. If a ransomware attack is detected, for instance, the system can automatically isolate the affected storage array from the rest of the network, preventing the spread of the malware. In addition to real-time threat detection, having a robust incident response plan in place is essential for mitigating the impact of a cyberattack and restoring normal operations as quickly as possible.

RAID also plays a role in maintaining system performance and reducing downtime during cyber incidents. In environments where high availability is crucial, RAID configurations that provide redundancy, such as RAID 10 or RAID 5, ensure that the system remains operational even if one or more drives are compromised or fail. This ensures that data remains accessible and that business operations can continue, even during an ongoing cyberattack or system failure. Furthermore, RAID's ability to quickly rebuild data from the remaining drives after a failure ensures that downtime is minimized, allowing organizations to maintain productivity while addressing the underlying security issue.

As organizations increasingly adopt hybrid cloud environments, the integration of RAID with cloud-based storage solutions presents additional opportunities for enhancing data security. Many cloud service providers offer built-in RAID configurations as part of their storage offerings, ensuring that data is protected against hardware failures and providing high availability. When combined with the security features of the cloud, such as encryption, access control, and real-time monitoring, RAID can further enhance the security of data stored offsite. Additionally, hybrid cloud environments enable organizations to leverage the scalability and flexibility of the cloud while maintaining the data redundancy and fault tolerance provided by RAID.

RAID continues to be a foundational technology for data protection, but its role in data security is evolving. While RAID provides essential protection against hardware failures and ensures data availability, it must be used in conjunction with other security measures to protect against cyber threats. As cyberattacks become more sophisticated, organizations must implement comprehensive data security strategies that combine the strengths of RAID with encryption, backups, access control, and advanced threat detection. By integrating RAID with these additional layers of security, organizations can ensure that their data remains safe and accessible, even in the face of increasingly complex and persistent cyber threats.

Disk I/O and RAID Performance Bottlenecks

In modern storage systems, disk input/output (I/O) operations are at the heart of performance optimization. I/O refers to the processes of reading from and writing to storage devices, and it is critical to ensuring that data is accessible when needed. RAID (Redundant Array of Independent Disks) is a technology widely used to improve disk I/O performance by utilizing multiple disks to distribute data across the array. While RAID provides significant benefits in terms of redundancy, fault tolerance, and performance, it is not immune to performance bottlenecks. Understanding the various factors that contribute to disk I/O bottlenecks and how they affect RAID performance is crucial for optimizing storage systems, particularly in high-demand environments where rapid data access is essential.

One of the main reasons RAID is used in disk I/O operations is its ability to distribute data across multiple disks, allowing for simultaneous read and write operations. By spreading data across different drives, RAID enables higher throughput and parallelism, which is particularly useful in high-performance computing (HPC), database systems, and virtualization environments. RAID 0, for example, strips data across multiple disks, allowing for faster read and write speeds by leveraging the combined throughput of all the disks in the array. However, this benefit is not without its challenges, as RAID systems can encounter performance bottlenecks under certain conditions that limit their ability to achieve optimal disk I/O performance.

A common source of RAID performance bottlenecks is the RAID controller itself. The RAID controller manages the distribution of data across the array, coordinates read and write operations, and ensures data integrity. If the RAID controller is not powerful enough to handle the demands of the system, it can become a performance bottleneck. This is particularly true in systems with large arrays or complex RAID configurations, such as RAID 5 and RAID 6, which require additional processing power to handle parity calculations. RAID controllers with insufficient processing power or limited cache can struggle to manage these operations efficiently, leading to slower disk I/O speeds. In high-performance systems, a hardware RAID controller with dedicated processing capabilities and cache memory is essential for maintaining optimal performance, as it offloads much of the work from the system's CPU and helps speed up I/O operations.

Another significant contributor to RAID performance bottlenecks is the disk itself. While RAID can improve overall system throughput by distributing data across multiple disks, the individual performance of the disks used in the RAID array can limit the speed at which data can be read or written. Traditional hard disk drives (HDDs), for instance, are mechanically limited in terms of speed, and they often suffer from higher latency and slower data access times compared to solid-state drives (SSDs). As the demand for faster disk I/O increases, using HDDs in RAID configurations may result in performance bottlenecks, especially in applications that require high-speed data access, such as databases, media servers, or virtualization environments. Upgrading to SSDs, which offer significantly faster read and write speeds, can help mitigate these bottlenecks and improve overall RAID performance, particularly in RAID 10 or RAID 0 configurations where high throughput is needed.

In addition to the limitations of individual disks, the RAID configuration itself can introduce performance bottlenecks. Certain RAID levels, such as RAID 5 and RAID 6, are designed to provide fault tolerance through parity, which requires additional computation during write operations. In RAID 5, for example, parity data is distributed across the drives in the array, and every write operation must calculate and update the parity. This process introduces an overhead that can slow down write performance, especially when the system is under heavy load. RAID 6 compounds this issue by requiring double parity, which increases the computational burden even further. While RAID 5 and RAID 6 offer excellent data protection, they can create performance bottlenecks, particularly in write-intensive applications where the system must continually update parity data.

To mitigate the impact of parity-related bottlenecks, some systems use techniques such as caching or write-back caches. In RAID systems with write-back cache, data is initially written to the cache and then written to the disk later. This can significantly improve write performance by reducing the number of I/O operations required during the write process. However, relying on cache memory can introduce risks if not properly managed. For example, in the event of a power failure, data in the cache may be lost before it is written to the disk, potentially resulting in data corruption. To address this issue, some RAID systems use battery-backed cache, which ensures that cached data is written to the disk even during power outages. While these techniques can help alleviate performance bottlenecks, they also add complexity to the system and must be carefully monitored to ensure data integrity.

Network-related bottlenecks are also a concern in RAID systems, especially in environments where storage is accessed over a network, such as in network-attached storage (NAS) or storage area networks (SAN). When RAID arrays are used in these environments, network latency and bandwidth limitations can introduce delays in data access, effectively slowing down disk I/O performance. The bandwidth of the network connecting the RAID array to the clients or servers is crucial to ensuring fast data access. If the network cannot handle the volume of data being requested or transmitted, it can become a bottleneck that limits the overall performance of the storage system. Upgrading to faster network interfaces, such as 10GbE or Fibre Channel, can help alleviate network-related bottlenecks and ensure that data flows smoothly between the storage system and the clients.

Another factor contributing to RAID I/O performance bottlenecks is the configuration of the storage array itself. Proper alignment of the RAID array is essential for achieving optimal performance. Misaligned partitions can result in additional read and write operations, leading to slower performance. This is especially true when dealing with modern storage devices, such as SSDs, where misalignment can have a significant impact on performance. Ensuring that the RAID array is properly configured and aligned can minimize unnecessary overhead and improve I/O performance.

In large-scale systems, the management and monitoring of RAID arrays also play a significant role in maintaining performance. Monitoring tools can provide real-time insights into the health of the RAID array, the status of individual disks, and the overall system performance. Administrators can use this data to proactively address potential issues, such as failing drives or imbalances in the array, before they lead to performance degradation. Additionally, as RAID arrays grow and expand, it is important to periodically reassess the system's performance and make adjustments as necessary. This may involve replacing older, slower drives, upgrading the RAID controller, or modifying the RAID configuration to optimize performance for changing workloads.

RAID systems are a powerful tool for optimizing disk I/O performance, but they are not without their challenges. Disk I/O bottlenecks in RAID arrays can arise from a variety of factors, including limitations of the RAID controller, the type of storage devices used, the RAID level chosen, and network-related issues. By understanding the factors that contribute to these bottlenecks and implementing strategies to mitigate them, businesses and organizations can maximize the performance of their RAID systems, ensuring fast and reliable data access in high-demand environments. Proper configuration, regular monitoring, and hardware upgrades are essential for maintaining optimal RAID performance and preventing I/O bottlenecks from negatively impacting system efficiency.

Energy Efficiency in RAID Systems

In the modern era of data storage, managing energy consumption is becoming increasingly important. As enterprises and data centers continue to grow, so does the demand for storage solutions that not only provide high performance and reliability but also minimize the environmental impact. RAID (Redundant Array of Independent Disks) systems, which have long been used for providing fault tolerance, improving performance, and ensuring data redundancy, are now also being scrutinized for their energy efficiency. The energy consumption of RAID systems is significant, particularly in large-scale deployments, where hundreds or thousands of hard drives or solid-state drives (SSDs) are used. The challenge is finding ways to reduce energy consumption in RAID arrays without compromising on the performance, redundancy, or availability that these systems are designed to provide.

One of the main factors influencing the energy efficiency of RAID systems is the type of storage media used. Traditional hard disk drives

(HDDs), which are mechanical in nature, consume more energy compared to their solid-state counterparts. HDDs have moving parts, such as spinning platters and read/write heads, which require power to operate. In contrast, solid-state drives (SSDs) use flash memory and have no moving parts, making them more energy-efficient. The lower power consumption of SSDs results from their ability to access data more quickly and with lower latency, meaning they can often complete tasks in less time than HDDs, thereby reducing the overall energy required for operations. As SSDs continue to decrease in price and improve in capacity, many RAID systems are transitioning to SSD-based configurations, providing a clear pathway to more energy-efficient storage solutions.

However, the shift from HDDs to SSDs does not automatically guarantee a significant reduction in energy consumption. While SSDs are more efficient in terms of power usage, RAID systems themselves can still be energy-intensive due to the need to manage multiple drives simultaneously. As RAID configurations grow in size to accommodate increasing data storage requirements, the overall energy consumption of the system can increase, particularly in configurations like RAID 5 and RAID 6, where multiple drives are needed to store data and parity information. The complexity of parity calculations, especially in RAID 5, increases the energy consumption associated with write operations. Similarly, in RAID 6, which uses dual parity, the energy cost of maintaining redundancy is even higher. Therefore, reducing the number of drives while maintaining the necessary redundancy is crucial for improving energy efficiency in these configurations.

In addition to the type of drives used, the RAID controller itself plays a significant role in the energy consumption of the system. RAID controllers are responsible for managing the data flow between the drives and coordinating read/write operations. Controllers that are not optimized for energy efficiency can contribute significantly to the overall power usage of a RAID system. Advanced RAID controllers, however, often come equipped with features like intelligent power management, which can reduce power consumption during idle periods or low-activity operations. For example, some RAID controllers allow for dynamic adjustments to the power usage based on the current workload, which helps to reduce energy consumption when the system is not under heavy load. Optimizing the RAID controller's settings for power efficiency can be a simple yet effective way to reduce the overall energy consumption of a RAID system.

Power management features within the drives themselves can also help to reduce the energy footprint of RAID systems. Modern drives, both HDDs and SSDs, often come with built-in power-saving modes. These modes allow the drives to enter a low-power state when they are not in use, such as when the system is idle or during periods of low I/O activity. By taking advantage of these features, RAID systems can minimize the power used during periods of inactivity, which can have a significant impact on energy consumption over time. Additionally, many enterprise-level storage devices now support more advanced power management features, such as automated spin-down for hard drives or the ability to reduce the operational power of SSDs when they are not actively being accessed. RAID administrators can configure these features within the system to optimize energy usage without sacrificing performance during active use.

One of the most effective ways to improve energy efficiency in RAID systems is to implement tiered storage strategies. In a tiered storage model, data is stored across different types of storage media based on the frequency of access. For example, frequently accessed data might be stored on high-performance SSDs, while less frequently accessed data could be stored on more power-efficient HDDs. By combining both types of drives in a single RAID system, businesses can strike a balance between performance and energy efficiency. The use of tiered storage reduces the need for all drives in the RAID array to operate at full capacity, allowing for significant reductions in energy consumption. Additionally, the intelligent distribution of data across multiple tiers ensures that high-energy drives are only used when necessary, while lower-energy drives handle the bulk of the storage workload.

Virtualization and cloud technologies are also contributing to the energy efficiency of RAID systems. With the rise of cloud computing, many businesses are moving their data storage needs to offsite cloud providers, where data can be stored in highly optimized data centers that are designed to minimize energy consumption. These data centers often implement energy-saving techniques such as server consolidation, cooling optimization, and the use of renewable energy sources. In a cloud environment, RAID technology is often used in conjunction with software-defined storage (SDS) systems, which allow for the dynamic allocation of storage resources based on workload requirements. This flexibility enables the cloud provider to optimize energy usage by distributing data across multiple storage devices in a way that minimizes power consumption. Virtualization, combined with RAID, allows organizations to make more efficient use of their storage resources, consolidating workloads and reducing the need for large numbers of dedicated physical servers and storage devices.

The ongoing trend towards sustainability in the IT industry is also influencing the development of energy-efficient RAID systems. As companies become more focused on reducing their carbon footprint, there is an increasing demand for storage solutions that consume less energy. RAID manufacturers are responding to this demand by developing energy-efficient controllers, drives, and storage systems that meet the growing need for both high performance and environmental responsibility. For example, some manufacturers are incorporating power-saving features into their RAID arrays, such as energy-efficient drive spinning, low-power idle modes, and improved cooling systems. These enhancements are helping organizations reduce their energy usage, lower operational costs, and contribute to sustainability goals.

RAID systems, like all storage solutions, must balance the need for performance, redundancy, and energy efficiency. As energy costs rise and environmental concerns become more prominent, the demand for power-efficient RAID configurations will only continue to grow. From the use of SSDs and intelligent RAID controllers to tiered storage models and virtualization, there are numerous ways to optimize energy consumption in RAID systems. By making thoughtful design choices and incorporating advanced technologies, organizations can significantly reduce the energy footprint of their storage systems without compromising on performance or data protection. This approach not only helps lower operational costs but also contributes to broader environmental sustainability efforts, making energy-efficient RAID systems a critical consideration for modern data storage solutions.

Comparing RAID with Other Data Protection Solutions

In the world of data storage and protection, RAID (Redundant Array of Independent Disks) has long been considered a fundamental technology for ensuring data redundancy, performance optimization, and fault tolerance. RAID works by combining multiple physical disks into a single logical unit, providing protection against hardware failures and increasing performance by distributing data across several drives. While RAID offers many advantages in terms of data protection, it is not the only solution available. Other data protection methods, such as traditional backups, cloud storage, and erasure coding, each have their own strengths and weaknesses. Comparing RAID with these alternatives is important for understanding which solution best meets the needs of different organizations and use cases.

RAID's primary strength lies in its ability to provide redundancy and fault tolerance. In configurations like RAID 1, RAID 5, and RAID 6, data is stored across multiple disks in such a way that if one disk fails, the data can still be accessed from the remaining disks. RAID 1, for example, mirrors data across two drives, meaning that both drives contain identical copies of the data. RAID 5 uses a combination of data striping and parity to distribute data and error-correcting information across multiple disks. RAID 6 takes this a step further by using double parity, enabling the system to tolerate the simultaneous failure of two drives. These configurations make RAID an excellent choice for environments that require high availability, such as databases, file servers, and other mission-critical systems.

However, RAID has its limitations. While it offers protection against hardware failure, it does not protect against other forms of data loss, such as human error, software bugs, malware, or ransomware attacks. For instance, if data is accidentally deleted or corrupted, RAID will simply mirror or distribute the corrupted data across the array, making it impossible to recover the original, uncorrupted version. RAID does not provide protection against cyber threats, which is where other data protection solutions come into play. In environments where data loss due to malware or accidental deletion is a significant concern, RAID may need to be complemented with additional solutions such as regular backups or cloud storage.

Backups are one of the most widely used data protection methods and serve as a fundamental tool for mitigating data loss. Unlike RAID, which is designed to protect data from hardware failure, backups provide a second copy of data that can be restored in the event of data corruption, accidental deletion, or cyberattacks. A backup system typically involves creating copies of data and storing them in a separate location, such as an external hard drive, network-attached storage (NAS), or cloud storage. Backups can be scheduled regularly to ensure that the most up-to-date versions of data are available for recovery. The main advantage of backups over RAID is that they provide an extra layer of protection against data corruption or malicious activity. If a file is deleted or corrupted, the backup allows for the restoration of the data to its previous state.

While backups are an essential part of any data protection strategy, they come with their own set of challenges. One significant drawback is that they can be time-consuming, particularly when dealing with large datasets. Restoring data from a backup can also take a significant amount of time, potentially leading to extended periods of downtime. Additionally, backup systems are often vulnerable to the same risks as the primary storage system, particularly if they are stored on-site. For example, in the event of a natural disaster or a physical break-in, both the primary storage and the backup data could be lost simultaneously. This is where offsite backups, such as cloud storage, come into play.

Cloud storage offers a scalable, flexible, and secure solution for data protection. By storing data in the cloud, organizations can ensure that their data is protected off-site, reducing the risk of losing both primary and backup copies of data due to physical threats. Cloud storage providers often implement advanced security measures, such as encryption and multi-factor authentication, to safeguard data against unauthorized access. Furthermore, cloud storage offers the benefit of accessibility from anywhere, enabling organizations to restore data quickly and efficiently, even in the event of a disaster. Cloud-based backup solutions typically provide automated backup schedules and versioning, ensuring that data is continuously protected without requiring manual intervention.

While cloud storage provides significant advantages in terms of accessibility and disaster recovery, it also has some drawbacks. The cost of cloud storage can add up over time, especially as storage requirements grow. Additionally, restoring large datasets from the cloud can be slower compared to local backups, depending on the internet speed and the size of the data being recovered. For this reason, some organizations opt for a hybrid approach, where critical data is backed up locally using RAID and non-critical data is backed up to the cloud. This approach allows for fast local recovery while still benefiting from the offsite protection offered by cloud storage.

Another emerging data protection solution that is gaining traction in the industry is erasure coding. Erasure coding is a technique used in distributed storage systems where data is broken into fragments, and redundant fragments are created and distributed across different storage devices. This technique provides a high level of fault tolerance and is often used in large-scale storage environments, such as cloud storage or object storage systems. Erasure coding offers several advantages over RAID, including improved storage efficiency and the ability to protect against multiple simultaneous drive failures. Unlike RAID, which typically uses mirrored or parity-based redundancy, erasure coding can tolerate a more significant number of failures without losing data. This makes it particularly useful for environments where data durability is a primary concern, such as in cloud storage providers or large-scale data centers.

However, erasure coding also has its limitations. It can introduce significant overhead, particularly in write-heavy workloads, as the system must calculate and distribute the redundant data across multiple devices. Additionally, erasure coding is more complex to implement and manage than traditional RAID, requiring specialized software and hardware. Despite these challenges, erasure coding offers an attractive alternative for organizations seeking higher storage efficiency and fault tolerance than what traditional RAID systems can provide.

When comparing RAID with other data protection solutions, it is clear that each method has its advantages and limitations. RAID excels in providing redundancy and fault tolerance at the disk level, but it does not address all potential causes of data loss, such as corruption or cyberattacks. Backups provide a crucial layer of protection, but they come with their own set of challenges, including the time required for data restoration and the risk of physical data loss. Cloud storage offers offsite protection and scalability, but it can be costly and slower for large-scale restores. Erasure coding presents a more efficient and fault-tolerant solution for distributed storage systems but is more complex to implement.

Ultimately, the most effective data protection strategy involves using a combination of these solutions. RAID can be used for ensuring hardware redundancy and performance, while backups, cloud storage, and erasure coding provide additional layers of protection against data loss from various causes. By leveraging the strengths of each solution, organizations can create a comprehensive data protection strategy that ensures data integrity, availability, and security, even in the face of hardware failures, cyber threats, and human error.

RAID in Virtualized Environments

Virtualized environments have become a cornerstone of modern IT infrastructures, offering flexibility, scalability, and improved resource utilization. These environments allow multiple virtual machines (VMs) to run on a single physical server, with each VM operating as an independent instance. This capability has revolutionized how enterprises manage their resources, offering significant advantages in terms of cost, efficiency, and ease of management. However, with the increase in virtualized workloads, there arises a need for robust data storage solutions that can handle the unique demands of virtual environments. RAID (Redundant Array of Independent Disks) is one such solution, playing a crucial role in ensuring data reliability, fault tolerance, and performance in these environments.

In a virtualized environment, data storage is a critical component because virtual machines often rely on large datasets, fast read and write speeds, and high availability. RAID offers multiple configurations that provide redundancy and improve performance by distributing data across multiple physical drives. The most common RAID levels used in virtualized environments are RAID 1, RAID 5, RAID 6, and

RAID 10. Each of these RAID configurations serves a different purpose, balancing the trade-off between data protection, performance, and storage capacity. By using RAID, virtualized environments can mitigate the risk of data loss due to hardware failures, ensure that VMs have consistent and fast access to data, and maintain system performance even in the event of drive failures.

RAID 1, or mirroring, is a RAID configuration where data is duplicated across two or more drives. In the event of a drive failure, the data is still available on the mirrored drive, ensuring high availability. This redundancy is essential in virtualized environments, where uptime is critical, and the failure of a single drive could result in service interruptions. RAID 1 offers excellent protection for mission-critical VMs, where data integrity and availability are of the utmost importance. However, it comes at the cost of storage efficiency because it essentially halves the usable storage capacity by storing identical copies of the data on each drive. In virtualized environments where cost-effective storage is a concern, this trade-off may limit the scalability of the system.

RAID 5 and RAID 6, which utilize striping with parity, are among the most commonly used RAID levels in virtualized environments that require a balance between fault tolerance and storage efficiency. RAID 5 uses data striping across multiple drives, with one drive's worth of space allocated to parity data. Parity allows the system to rebuild data if a single drive fails, making it a cost-effective solution for providing fault tolerance without sacrificing too much storage capacity. RAID 6 is similar to RAID 5 but adds an extra layer of protection with two parity blocks, allowing for the failure of two drives without data loss. RAID 6 is typically preferred in environments where the risk of multiple drive failures is higher, or where extra protection is necessary.

In virtualized environments, RAID 5 and RAID 6 are especially useful because they provide a good balance between storage efficiency, redundancy, and performance. They can handle large volumes of data with reduced redundancy overhead compared to RAID 1, making them ideal for systems that need to store significant amounts of data, such as virtualized file servers or large-scale databases. However, both RAID 5 and RAID 6 can suffer from performance bottlenecks during write-intensive operations due to the parity calculations required for each write. Virtualized environments that rely heavily on write operations, such as transactional databases or virtual desktop infrastructures (VDI), may experience slower performance with RAID 5 or RAID 6.

RAID 10, which combines the benefits of RAID 1 and RAID 0, is another popular configuration in virtualized environments. RAID 10 provides both redundancy and high performance by mirroring data and striping it across multiple drives. This means that in the event of a drive failure, data can be accessed from the mirrored copy, ensuring high availability, while the striping improves performance by allowing for parallel read and write operations. RAID 10 is well-suited for virtualized environments that require both high performance and redundancy, such as virtual machines running resource-intensive applications. However, RAID 10 sacrifices storage efficiency, as it requires twice the amount of disk space for the data being stored. While this can be an expensive option in terms of disk usage, the performance benefits it offers often outweigh the cost in high-performance virtualized environments.

In virtualized environments, the storage system must be able to provide fast, reliable access to data while supporting the dynamic nature of virtual machines. As VMs are created, moved, and destroyed frequently in virtual environments, the underlying storage system must be able to accommodate these changes without affecting performance or availability. RAID systems can be used in conjunction with virtualized storage solutions such as Storage Area Networks (SANs) or Network-Attached Storage (NAS) to provide centralized storage that is optimized for virtualization. These storage solutions allow for the centralized management of multiple RAID arrays, ensuring that virtual machines can access storage resources efficiently and reliably. The use of RAID in combination with SAN or NAS technologies enables virtualized environments to scale efficiently, supporting growing storage needs while ensuring that data is readily available and protected.

Another important consideration when using RAID in virtualized environments is the need for performance optimization. RAID systems that use SSDs in place of traditional hard drives can significantly improve I/O performance. SSDs provide faster data access speeds and lower latency, which is particularly important in virtualized environments where multiple VMs may be accessing data simultaneously. The use of SSDs in RAID configurations can provide higher throughput and reduce the time required for VMs to access data. However, SSDs can be more expensive than traditional hard drives, and the trade-off between cost and performance must be carefully considered when designing a storage system for a virtualized environment.

Storage virtualization is another key aspect of modern virtualized environments, and it plays a significant role in RAID's role within these systems. Storage virtualization abstracts the physical storage hardware from the virtual machines, allowing them to interact with a logical pool of storage resources rather than individual disks. This abstraction enables more efficient storage management, as virtual machines can be moved between physical hosts without requiring manual data migration. RAID systems can be integrated with storage virtualization platforms to provide a layer of data redundancy and performance optimization for virtualized storage. This integration ensures that the underlying RAID configuration is transparent to the virtual machines, providing high availability and fault tolerance without complicating the management of virtualized resources.

As virtualized environments continue to grow and evolve, the need for efficient, high-performing storage systems that can handle large amounts of dynamic data becomes increasingly critical. RAID remains a fundamental technology for ensuring data protection, high availability, and performance in these environments. The ongoing advancements in storage technologies, such as SSDs, storage virtualization, and software-defined storage, are further enhancing the role of RAID in modern IT infrastructures. By providing flexibility, scalability, and redundancy, RAID will continue to play a key role in ensuring that virtualized environments can meet the ever-growing demands of modern computing while maintaining data integrity and availability.

RAID for Media and Entertainment Applications

The media and entertainment industry relies heavily on high-quality, high-volume data storage and rapid access to large files. The shift from traditional film and tape to digital formats has led to an explosion in the amount of data generated and used in everything from video production to animation, special effects, and post-production workflows. For these industries, having reliable and efficient storage solutions is crucial, and RAID (Redundant Array of Independent Disks) has become a key technology for meeting the demanding needs of media and entertainment applications. By combining multiple hard drives or solid-state drives into a single logical unit, RAID provides redundancy, performance optimization, and fault tolerance—features that are essential in the high-pressure, time-sensitive environment of media production.

One of the primary reasons RAID is used in media and entertainment applications is to address the need for high-performance storage. Video editing, visual effects, and 3D rendering applications require fast read and write speeds to handle large video files, image sequences, and complex projects. RAID systems can provide significant performance benefits by distributing data across multiple drives, allowing multiple I/O operations to occur in parallel. For instance, in a RAID 0 configuration, data is striped across two or more drives, enabling faster access to the data by utilizing the combined throughput of all the drives in the array. RAID 0 is often used in scenarios where speed is a priority, such as in the early stages of video editing or rendering, where large video files need to be accessed and manipulated quickly. However, RAID 0 offers no redundancy, meaning that if one drive fails, all data in the array is lost, making it unsuitable for critical applications where data integrity is paramount.

For applications in media and entertainment where data integrity is just as important as performance, RAID 1, which mirrors data across two or more drives, is often preferred. In RAID 1, every piece of data is duplicated, ensuring that if one drive fails, the data is still available from the mirrored drive. This redundancy makes RAID 1 an ideal choice for environments where reliability is critical, such as in video post-production or audio recording, where losing data could result in expensive setbacks or delays. While RAID 1 provides fault tolerance, it does so at the cost of storage efficiency, as the usable capacity is effectively halved due to the mirrored nature of the array. Despite this, the protection it offers for crucial data often outweighs the storage cost in environments where uptime is essential.

RAID 5 and RAID 6 are more commonly used in larger-scale media and entertainment environments, where data needs to be both highly available and protected from hardware failures. RAID 5 uses a combination of striping and parity to distribute data and parity information across three or more drives. In the event of a single drive failure, the system can still function by using the parity data to rebuild the lost information. RAID 6 extends the protection of RAID 5 by using dual parity, which allows it to tolerate the failure of two drives simultaneously. This makes RAID 6 particularly useful in large media storage systems where the failure of a single drive could otherwise disrupt the entire production process. By offering redundancy without the high overhead of full mirroring, RAID 5 and RAID 6 provide a good balance of fault tolerance and storage efficiency, which is particularly beneficial for large video libraries, asset management, or content storage in media companies.

In media and entertainment applications, the scale of the data storage infrastructure is also an important consideration. High-definition (HD), 4K, and 8K video formats have become the standard in media production, resulting in massive storage requirements. RAID systems can be scaled to meet these growing demands by adding additional drives to the array, allowing storage to expand as the need for higher capacity increases. The ability to add drives to a RAID array without significant downtime or disruption makes RAID a flexible solution for media organizations that require scalability. Furthermore, the growing use of SSDs (solid-state drives) in RAID configurations is helping to meet the performance demands of modern media production. SSDs provide faster data access speeds, lower latency, and improved durability compared to traditional hard drives, which significantly enhances the overall performance of RAID arrays. SSD-based RAID systems are becoming increasingly popular in video editing and post-production environments, where high-speed access to large files is essential for efficient workflows.

RAID is also a key component of network-attached storage (NAS) and storage area networks (SAN), which are commonly used in media and entertainment applications for centralized storage. NAS and SAN solutions enable multiple users to access shared storage resources over a network, facilitating collaboration among teams working on large projects. RAID is often integrated into these systems to ensure that data is both readily available and protected from hardware failure. For example, in a SAN environment, RAID 5 or RAID 6 configurations are often used to provide high-capacity, high-availability storage that can be accessed by multiple workstations in a production studio. Similarly, RAID 10 or RAID 1 arrays may be used in NAS systems to provide fast access to smaller-scale projects or to serve as backup storage for critical data.

Moreover, RAID systems in media and entertainment applications are also closely tied to the concept of data protection and disaster recovery. The fast-paced nature of media production means that projects are often under tight deadlines, and any disruption in the availability of data can lead to costly delays. RAID helps mitigate this risk by ensuring that data is available even in the event of a hardware failure. However, RAID alone is not sufficient for comprehensive data protection. In addition to RAID, many media and entertainment companies implement regular backup strategies, often utilizing offsite or cloud-based backups to protect data from disasters such as fires, floods, or theft. Combining RAID with backup systems allows for the recovery of data in the event of catastrophic failures that RAID alone cannot address.

For example, in a post-production environment where multiple video editing suites are working on the same project, RAID systems provide the necessary redundancy to ensure that work can continue seamlessly if a drive fails. However, to safeguard against the loss of entire projects due to ransomware, user error, or physical damage to the storage hardware, companies often implement cloud-based backups or replicated storage in geographically dispersed data centers. These additional layers of data protection ensure that media assets remain safe, even if a primary RAID array becomes compromised or damaged.

RAID is a cornerstone of data protection in media and entertainment applications, providing essential redundancy and performance optimization. Whether used in video editing, animation, visual effects, or media archiving, RAID enables faster data access, protects against hardware failures, and ensures that large-scale data operations run smoothly. As the demands for higher-resolution media, faster production timelines, and larger-scale data storage continue to increase, RAID remains a crucial technology in the media and entertainment industry. Its ability to deliver fault tolerance, performance, and scalability ensures that creative professionals can continue to produce high-quality content while safeguarding their data.

RAID in Database Management Systems

Database management systems (DBMS) are critical components in modern IT infrastructure, managing and organizing data for fast retrieval, modification, and storage. These systems are used across various industries, handling massive amounts of data with high transaction rates and complex query processing. The reliability, performance, and availability of a DBMS are paramount, especially in mission-critical applications where even minor downtime or data loss can have significant financial and operational consequences. RAID (Redundant Array of Independent Disks) plays an integral role in ensuring that database management systems meet these demands. By utilizing multiple disks to enhance data availability, improve performance, and provide fault tolerance, RAID enables DBMS environments to maintain the high levels of data integrity and uptime required for critical operations.

In a typical database environment, data storage is a crucial component that directly affects the performance of the system. A DBMS relies on fast read and write operations to process large volumes of data quickly. RAID systems are designed to optimize these I/O operations by spreading data across multiple physical drives. In this way, RAID not only enhances the speed of data access but also ensures that data is distributed in a manner that minimizes the risk of data loss due to hardware failure. For example, in RAID 0, data is striped across multiple disks, allowing for faster read and write speeds by accessing different portions of the data in parallel. RAID 0 is often used in situations where high throughput is required, such as in the temporary storage of large data sets or in environments where performance is the priority over data redundancy.

However, RAID 0 offers no redundancy or fault tolerance, making it unsuitable for database environments where data integrity and availability are critical. In these cases, RAID 1, which mirrors data across two or more drives, is often preferred. RAID 1 provides redundancy by ensuring that each piece of data is stored on two or more drives, creating an identical copy of the data. If one drive fails, the system can continue operating using the mirrored copy, ensuring that there is no data loss and minimal disruption. This makes RAID 1 a suitable choice for smaller databases or transactional systems where reliability and fault tolerance are prioritized over storage efficiency. The drawback of RAID 1 is its reduced storage efficiency, as the total usable capacity is half of the combined capacity of the drives.

In larger database management systems, where scalability and storage efficiency are more important, RAID 5 and RAID 6 are often used. RAID 5 offers a good balance between performance, storage efficiency, and fault tolerance. It stripes data across multiple drives and distributes parity information, which is used to rebuild data if a single drive fails. The parity data is spread across the drives, meaning that only one drive's worth of storage is used for redundancy, making RAID 5 more storage-efficient than RAID 1. In the event of a drive failure, the data can be reconstructed using the parity information, allowing the system to continue functioning until the failed drive is replaced. RAID 6 extends the concept of RAID 5 by using two sets of parity data instead of one, enabling the system to tolerate the simultaneous failure of two drives. While RAID 6 offers enhanced fault tolerance, it comes with an additional overhead for storing the extra parity data, which reduces the overall usable capacity compared to RAID 5.

RAID 5 and RAID 6 are popular choices in database management systems, particularly in environments where read-heavy operations, such as data warehousing and analytical queries, are common. These RAID levels provide a good balance of performance and redundancy, making them ideal for environments where data protection is essential but the overhead of full mirroring (like in RAID 1 or RAID 10) is not feasible due to storage constraints. Both RAID 5 and RAID 6 allow databases to handle large transaction volumes while still ensuring that data can be quickly rebuilt in the event of a drive failure. However, these configurations can suffer from performance bottlenecks during write operations, particularly in systems with heavy transactional workloads. The need to calculate and update parity data during writes can introduce latency, which is why some DBMS environments opt for alternative RAID configurations, such as RAID 10, when performance is the primary concern.

RAID 10, which combines the features of RAID 1 and RAID 0, is often used in high-performance database management systems where both redundancy and speed are critical. RAID 10 mirrors data across pairs of drives and then stripes the mirrored pairs, providing both redundancy and improved performance. This configuration provides excellent fault tolerance because data is mirrored, and high performance due to striping. RAID 10 is particularly effective in environments with high write operations, such as online transaction processing (OLTP) systems, where database consistency and high transaction throughput are required. However, like RAID 1, RAID 10 is less storage-efficient because it requires twice the amount of disk space for the mirrored data. Despite the cost, the combination of performance and redundancy makes RAID 10 an attractive option for demanding DBMS workloads.

One of the challenges that database administrators face when using RAID in DBMS environments is balancing performance with redundancy. In environments that require high availability and fault tolerance, the overhead introduced by RAID configurations like RAID 5 and RAID 6—particularly during write-heavy operations—can be detrimental to system performance. As a result, many modern DBMS environments employ hybrid storage solutions that combine RAID with other performance optimization techniques, such as caching, tiered storage, and the use of solid-state drives (SSDs). SSDs are particularly effective in improving the performance of RAID arrays because they offer significantly faster data access speeds and lower latency than traditional hard disk drives (HDDs). By using SSDs in conjunction with RAID configurations like RAID 10 or RAID 5, DBMS environments can achieve high throughput while maintaining the redundancy required for data protection.

Another consideration in RAID-based DBMS environments is the role of the RAID controller. The RAID controller manages the data distribution across the array and coordinates the read/write operations between the drives. In high-performance database environments, it is critical that the RAID controller is capable of handling the system's workload efficiently. RAID controllers with advanced features, such as hardware-based parity calculations, dedicated cache memory, and support for multiple drive interfaces, can significantly improve the overall performance of the RAID array. In high-demand environments, using a hardware RAID controller that offloads data management tasks from the server's main processor can enhance system responsiveness and ensure that the database can handle large volumes of transactions without lag.

In conclusion, RAID plays an essential role in the design and operation of database management systems by providing fault tolerance, performance optimization, and scalability. Whether through RAID 1's mirroring for small transactional databases, RAID 5's cost-effective parity protection for larger databases, or RAID 10's combination of speed and redundancy for high-performance applications, RAID configurations are an integral part of modern database infrastructures. As databases continue to grow in size and complexity, RAID will remain a vital tool for ensuring that these systems are both reliable and efficient, helping organizations protect their data while ensuring high levels of availability and performance.

Enterprise-Level RAID: Best Practices for Scalability

As businesses grow and data requirements become more complex, enterprise-level RAID (Redundant Array of Independent Disks) systems must be able to scale efficiently while maintaining high performance and reliability. Scalability is critical in enterprise environments where storage needs evolve rapidly due to factors such as data growth, new applications, and changing technological requirements. RAID technology, when implemented properly, offers a flexible, high-performing, and reliable solution for large-scale storage systems. However, to ensure that RAID can support an enterprise's ever-expanding infrastructure, it is essential to follow best practices that focus on optimizing performance, capacity, redundancy, and ease of management.

One of the most important considerations for scalability in enterprise-level RAID systems is the choice of RAID level. Different RAID configurations offer varying levels of redundancy, performance, and storage efficiency, and selecting the right RAID level for the given workload is crucial for ensuring long-term scalability. For example, RAID 10, which combines the redundancy of RAID 1 (mirroring) and the performance benefits of RAID 0 (striping), is often used in environments that require high availability and high throughput. However, while RAID 10 provides excellent performance and fault tolerance, it can be inefficient in terms of storage utilization because it requires twice the number of drives for mirroring. RAID 5 and RAID 6, on the other hand, provide more efficient storage utilization by using parity to protect data. RAID 5 can tolerate a single drive failure, while RAID 6 offers additional protection with double parity, allowing for two simultaneous drive failures without data loss. Both RAID 5 and RAID 6 offer a balance between fault tolerance, storage efficiency, and performance, making them suitable for large-scale environments that need to maximize storage capacity while maintaining redundancy.

In enterprise environments, RAID systems need to support both large volumes of data and high transaction rates. The sheer scale of enterprise storage environments means that a RAID system must be capable of handling multiple terabytes (or even petabytes) of data across hundreds or thousands of drives. This requires a well-thought-out strategy for expanding the RAID array as storage needs grow. One common approach to scalability is to use modular storage systems that allow additional drives to be added without disrupting operations. These modular systems are designed to be easily expanded, either by adding new drives to existing arrays or by adding entirely new storage enclosures to the system. This flexibility ensures that the RAID system can grow alongside the business, accommodating new data requirements without requiring a complete system overhaul.

Another important factor in ensuring the scalability of enterprise-level RAID systems is the use of enterprise-grade RAID controllers. RAID controllers are responsible for managing the RAID array, ensuring that data is correctly distributed across the drives and maintaining parity calculations in the case of RAID 5 and RAID 6 configurations. In high-demand environments, it is essential that RAID controllers are able to handle the volume of data being processed without introducing latency. Enterprise-grade RAID controllers are designed to support large-scale storage systems and offer features such as high-speed data throughput, enhanced cache memory, support for multiple drives, and advanced error correction. Some controllers also feature built-in management tools that allow administrators to monitor the health of the array, identify potential issues before they become problems, and automate tasks such as drive rebuilding and expansion. Choosing a high-performance RAID controller is key to ensuring that the system can handle both the current and future data demands of the organization.

Another best practice for scalable RAID in enterprise environments is optimizing storage for performance through tiered storage architectures. In tiered storage systems, data is classified based on its importance and frequency of access. Frequently accessed data, or "hot" data, is placed on high-performance storage devices, such as solid-state drives (SSDs), while less frequently accessed data, or "cold" data, is moved to slower but more cost-effective storage media, such as hard disk drives (HDDs). RAID systems can be implemented across different storage tiers, allowing the organization to take full advantage of the performance of SSDs while ensuring that storage costs are kept manageable by using cheaper drives for less critical data. This tiered approach ensures that enterprise RAID systems can scale effectively while providing the necessary performance for critical applications and minimizing costs for archival or backup storage.

Data protection and redundancy are paramount in enterprise storage systems, and RAID configurations must ensure that data is not only scalable but also highly available. As businesses rely on their data for critical operations, downtime or data loss can result in severe financial and operational consequences. RAID provides redundancy by using multiple disks to store copies of data, but enterprise systems often require additional protection. For example, RAID can be combined with replication technologies that create copies of data across multiple geographical locations, ensuring that if one data center experiences a failure, the data can still be accessed from another location. This additional level of protection, often referred to as geo-redundancy, ensures that data remains available even in the event of a localized disaster or hardware failure. In high-availability environments, it is also common to implement hot spares—additional drives that remain idle until a failure occurs—so that the RAID array can be rebuilt automatically without manual intervention.

Managing the complexity of large-scale RAID systems in an enterprise environment is another critical aspect of scalability. As the size of the storage system increases, so too does the complexity of managing and maintaining it. RAID arrays with hundreds or thousands of drives require a robust management framework to ensure that the system is functioning optimally. This is where storage management software comes into play. Enterprise-grade storage management tools allow administrators to monitor the health of individual drives, manage storage pools, track performance metrics, and handle fault recovery. These tools also provide automated alerts to inform administrators when a drive is nearing failure or when the system is approaching capacity limits. By using storage management software, enterprises can streamline RAID management, ensuring that the system remains scalable and efficient as data grows.

In addition to software tools, enterprises often employ data lifecycle management (DLM) policies to help manage data growth within the RAID system. DLM strategies ensure that data is properly archived, deleted, or migrated according to its importance or relevance over time. For example, data that is no longer actively used can be archived to slower, less expensive storage media, while more important or frequently accessed data remains on high-performance storage. By incorporating DLM practices into RAID-based storage architectures, organizations can ensure that their systems remain scalable and cost-effective, avoiding unnecessary data bloat and over-provisioning.

As enterprises continue to evolve and their storage needs grow, RAID technology must be flexible enough to support changing requirements. By following best practices for scalability, including selecting the appropriate RAID level, using enterprise-grade RAID controllers, implementing tiered storage systems, ensuring data redundancy through replication, and utilizing effective storage management tools, organizations can create RAID systems that scale with the business. The ability to expand storage capacity without disrupting operations, while maintaining high performance, reliability, and data protection, is crucial for supporting the ongoing success of the enterprise. RAID will continue to play a pivotal role in ensuring that businesses can meet their data storage needs, now and in the future, as they face an ever-expanding data landscape.

RAID and Storage Tiering: Improving Performance

In the ever-evolving landscape of data storage, one of the key challenges faced by organizations is how to efficiently manage large volumes of data while ensuring high performance and cost-effectiveness. As data grows in size and complexity, it becomes increasingly important to optimize how data is stored, accessed, and retrieved. RAID (Redundant Array of Independent Disks) and storage tiering are two crucial technologies that, when combined, can dramatically improve the performance, scalability, and efficiency of data storage systems. RAID provides redundancy and fault tolerance, while storage tiering optimizes how data is distributed across different types of storage devices based on its access frequency. By leveraging both RAID and storage tiering, organizations can ensure that their storage systems are not only secure and reliable but also fast and cost-effective.

RAID technology enhances storage performance by distributing data across multiple disks, which enables concurrent access to different portions of data. The performance gains that RAID can offer depend on the specific RAID configuration employed. For instance, RAID 0, which stripes data across multiple disks, can significantly improve performance by allowing multiple I/O operations to be performed simultaneously. However, RAID 0 offers no redundancy, so the risk of data loss is high if a single drive fails. On the other hand, RAID 1, which mirrors data across two or more disks, provides redundancy but may not deliver the same performance boost as RAID 0. For many enterprise environments, RAID 5 or RAID 6 configurations are often used, as they offer a balance between performance, fault tolerance, and storage efficiency. These configurations utilize parity to allow for data recovery in the event of a drive failure, while also improving read performance by distributing the data across multiple disks.

While RAID provides performance enhancements through its data distribution and redundancy mechanisms, it is not sufficient on its own to meet the growing demands of modern storage environments. One of the key limitations of traditional RAID configurations is that they typically treat all data the same, regardless of how frequently it is accessed. For instance, data that is frequently accessed might be stored on the same type of storage as data that is rarely accessed. This can lead to inefficiencies, as the storage system may allocate high-performance resources to data that doesn't require fast access, while neglecting to prioritize data that is crucial for the organization's day-to-day operations.

This is where storage tiering comes into play. Storage tiering is the practice of classifying data based on its access frequency or importance and then storing it on different types of storage devices accordingly. For example, frequently accessed data, such as active database tables or high-demand files, can be stored on high-performance storage media like solid-state drives (SSDs), which offer faster read and write speeds than traditional hard disk drives (HDDs). Less frequently accessed data, such as archival or backup data, can be stored on slower, less expensive storage media like HDDs. By dynamically moving data between different storage tiers based on its usage patterns, organizations can optimize storage costs and performance, ensuring that critical data is always available when needed without wasting valuable resources on less important data.

Combining RAID with storage tiering allows organizations to leverage the benefits of both technologies. RAID can be used to ensure data redundancy and fault tolerance, while storage tiering can optimize how data is stored across different types of drives. For instance, a RAID 10 array could be used for high-performance workloads where both redundancy and speed are crucial, and the most frequently accessed data could be stored on SSDs within the RAID array. Less critical data could be placed on a separate RAID 5 array that uses HDDs, providing a more cost-effective solution for less performance-intensive workloads. This combination of RAID and storage tiering ensures that the storage system can scale to meet the needs of a growing organization, providing fast access to critical data while minimizing costs associated with less frequently accessed information.

In addition to improving performance and cost efficiency, RAID and storage tiering can also enhance overall system reliability. In traditional systems without tiering, all data is treated equally, which means that the performance of the entire system can be compromised if a significant portion of the data is stored on slower, older devices. With storage tiering, however, high-performance resources are reserved for the most important and frequently accessed data, reducing the risk of bottlenecks that can occur when a system relies too heavily on slower storage. Additionally, by using RAID to provide redundancy across all storage tiers, data remains protected, ensuring high availability even if a drive fails within one of the tiers.

One of the challenges associated with implementing RAID and storage tiering is the complexity of managing data across multiple storage devices and configurations. As the amount of data grows and storage requirements become more complex, it becomes increasingly important to have robust storage management tools that can automate the movement of data between tiers, monitor the health of the drives, and ensure that the system remains optimized. Modern storage management solutions often include features such as automated tiering, where data is moved between different storage media based on predefined policies or real-time access patterns. For example, data that has not been accessed for a certain period can be automatically moved from high-performance SSD storage to slower HDD storage. By automating this process, organizations can reduce the administrative overhead associated with managing data across multiple tiers and ensure that their storage systems remain efficient and responsive.

The integration of RAID with storage tiering is particularly valuable in environments that handle large-scale data workloads, such as in big data analytics, video editing, and high-performance computing. These environments require fast, reliable access to vast amounts of data, and without proper optimization, the performance of the storage system can quickly become a limiting factor. By implementing RAID in combination with storage tiering, organizations can ensure that data is stored in the most appropriate location based on its importance and access frequency, improving both the speed and efficiency of their storage systems. This approach not only improves the performance of data-intensive applications but also ensures that the organization's storage resources are utilized effectively, minimizing costs and reducing unnecessary overhead.

In summary, combining RAID with storage tiering provides a powerful solution for improving performance, scalability, and cost efficiency in modern storage environments. RAID ensures that data is protected from hardware failure through redundancy, while storage tiering optimizes the allocation of resources based on access frequency, ensuring that critical data is stored on high-performance media and less important data is stored on more cost-effective devices. This approach not only improves the overall efficiency of the storage system but also enables organizations to scale their storage solutions in a way that meets the demands of growing data workloads. As organizations continue to generate and rely on larger volumes of data, the integration of RAID and storage tiering will remain essential for maintaining high-performance, reliable, and cost-effective storage systems.

RAID and Data Integrity: Detecting Errors Early

In today's digital age, where businesses and organizations rely heavily on data for decision-making, operations, and innovation, ensuring the integrity of this data is more important than ever. Data integrity refers to the accuracy, consistency, and reliability of data throughout its lifecycle. Data corruption or loss can have disastrous consequences, ranging from minor operational disruptions to catastrophic data breaches and system failures. RAID (Redundant Array of Independent Disks) systems are designed to address these concerns by improving data redundancy, fault tolerance, and overall system reliability. One of the critical roles of RAID technology is to detect and correct errors early, preventing data corruption from escalating and ensuring that data remains intact and accessible when needed.

RAID enhances data integrity primarily through its fault tolerance mechanisms. By using multiple disks to store data and employing techniques like striping, mirroring, and parity, RAID systems ensure that even in the event of a hardware failure, data can be reconstructed and remains available. In configurations such as RAID 1, data is mirrored across two or more drives, creating an exact replica of the data on each disk. If one drive fails, the system can continue operating using the mirrored copy, ensuring that no data is lost. Similarly, in RAID 5 and RAID 6, parity data is distributed across the array, providing a mechanism for recovering lost data in the event of a single or double drive failure. While RAID's primary focus is on data redundancy, it also plays a crucial role in detecting and mitigating errors before they can compromise the integrity of the data.

One of the key benefits of RAID in maintaining data integrity is its ability to detect and correct errors at the hardware level. In systems like RAID 5 and RAID 6, parity is calculated for each block of data stored on the array. The parity data is stored across the disks along with the original data, and in the event of a failure, the system can use the parity information to rebuild the lost data. This redundancy not only provides fault tolerance but also ensures that if data becomes corrupted or an error occurs, it can be detected early during the rebuild process. The parity mechanism allows the system to cross-check the data and verify that it is accurate. If an error is detected, the system can automatically repair the affected data using the parity information, preventing data corruption from spreading or going undetected.

In addition to parity, many RAID controllers also incorporate error-correcting codes (ECC), which help detect and correct errors in real-time as data is written or read from the array. ECC is particularly useful in ensuring the integrity of data by preventing single-bit errors from corrupting large blocks of data. When a RAID system uses ECC, it can detect and correct errors on the fly, allowing for quick remediation before the data is compromised. For example, if a single bit of data becomes corrupted during a write operation, the ECC can identify the error and correct it before the data is committed to the disk. This form of error detection and correction is particularly important in environments where data integrity is paramount, such as financial institutions, healthcare organizations, and cloud storage providers, where even the smallest error can have significant consequences.

RAID also plays a role in detecting and correcting errors in the storage media itself. Hard drives and SSDs are prone to wear and tear, and over time, sectors of the disk can become unreadable or start to degrade. RAID systems continuously monitor the health of the individual drives within the array and can identify failing drives before they cause data loss. For example, most modern RAID controllers use S.M.A.R.T. (Self-Monitoring, Analysis, and Reporting Technology) to track the health of each drive in the array. S.M.A.R.T. collects data on various parameters, such as the temperature of the drive, the number of read/write errors, and the number of bad sectors. By continuously monitoring these parameters, the RAID system can detect early signs of impending failure, such as increased error rates or mechanical issues with the drive. If a drive is detected to be failing, the RAID system can alert the administrator, allowing them to replace the faulty drive before any data is lost. This proactive approach helps prevent catastrophic data corruption and ensures that data remains protected throughout its lifecycle.

Another critical feature of RAID systems in maintaining data integrity is their ability to perform regular integrity checks. Many RAID systems include features that allow the administrator to schedule periodic consistency checks, where the system verifies the integrity of the data across the array. These checks can be configured to run at regular intervals or during periods of low system activity, ensuring that any potential errors are detected before they affect data access or cause corruption. During these checks, the system compares the data stored on each drive with the corresponding parity or mirrored copy, and if any inconsistencies are found, the system can attempt to repair them using the redundant data. This process is essential for ensuring that data remains consistent and accurate over time, particularly in large storage environments where data corruption can go unnoticed for long periods.

RAID's role in detecting errors early is particularly important in environments that deal with large volumes of transactional data, such as databases or e-commerce platforms. In these environments, data consistency is crucial, and even a minor error can lead to significant disruptions in service. RAID ensures that data can be quickly recovered in the event of a failure, reducing the risk of downtime and maintaining the integrity of business operations. For example, in a financial system, a single corrupted transaction record can lead to incorrect financial reporting, customer dissatisfaction, or regulatory non-compliance. RAID systems, by maintaining data integrity and allowing for the rapid detection and correction of errors, prevent such issues from arising, ensuring that businesses can continue to operate without interruption.

While RAID provides significant benefits for data integrity, it is important to note that RAID alone cannot guarantee complete protection against all forms of data corruption or loss. For example, RAID does not protect against software bugs, malware, or user errors that can lead to data corruption. To address these risks, RAID systems must be integrated with other data protection strategies, such as regular backups, encryption, and access controls. Backups ensure that copies of data are available for recovery in the event of a catastrophic failure, while encryption protects data from unauthorized access and tampering. Access controls and monitoring tools can help prevent human errors and malicious activity that might compromise the integrity of the data.

RAID plays an essential role in ensuring data integrity by detecting errors early and providing mechanisms for error correction. By employing redundancy through parity and mirroring, RAID systems help maintain the accuracy and availability of data even in the event of hardware failures. The incorporation of error-correcting codes, S.M.A.R.T. monitoring, and regular consistency checks further enhances RAID's ability to detect issues before they escalate into more serious problems. In environments where data integrity is critical, such as in financial services, healthcare, and cloud storage, RAID provides an essential layer of protection that ensures data remains reliable and accessible. However, RAID should always be part of a broader data protection strategy that includes backups, encryption, and access control to address the full spectrum of potential risks to data integrity.

RAID Failure Modes and Prevention Strategies

RAID (Redundant Array of Independent Disks) has long been a cornerstone of modern data storage, offering both performance optimization and data redundancy to protect against hardware failures. Despite its many advantages, RAID is not immune to failure. RAID arrays, like any technology, are subject to various failure modes that can compromise the integrity of data. Understanding these failure modes and implementing effective prevention strategies is critical to maintaining the reliability and availability of data in enterprise environments. By recognizing potential issues and preparing appropriate measures to mitigate them, businesses can ensure the continued performance and security of their RAID systems.

RAID failure modes can generally be classified into two broad categories: hardware failures and logical failures. Hardware failures are related to physical components, such as disks, RAID controllers, or cables, while logical failures refer to issues with the data stored within the RAID array itself, including corruption or loss of data integrity. Each of these failure modes has its own set of risks and challenges, and understanding how to prevent or mitigate them is essential for the successful operation of RAID-based storage systems.

One of the most common failure modes in RAID systems is the failure of a single hard drive. In RAID configurations like RAID 1, RAID 5, and RAID 6, data is stored across multiple drives, with redundancy provided through mirroring or parity. While these configurations offer fault tolerance, they are not immune to individual drive failures. In the event of a single drive failure, RAID is designed to continue operating in a degraded state, where the system can still access the data using the remaining drives or parity information. However, this degraded state poses significant risks, as the array becomes vulnerable to additional failures. If another drive fails during the rebuild process, the data could be lost, as the RAID array no longer has sufficient redundancy to recover the lost data. This situation highlights the importance of maintaining a proactive approach to RAID management by constantly monitoring drive health and replacing failed drives as soon as possible.

Another failure mode that can occur in RAID systems is the failure of the RAID controller. The RAID controller is responsible for managing the array, coordinating read and write operations, and handling data reconstruction in the event of a failure. A failure of the RAID controller can result in the entire array becoming inaccessible, rendering data temporarily or permanently unavailable. RAID controllers are susceptible to failures due to hardware defects, firmware bugs, or power surges. In such cases, the failure of the RAID controller can lead to data loss or corruption, especially if the controller cannot effectively manage the rebuild process or if it is unable to recover parity data correctly. To prevent controller failures, it is essential to regularly update firmware and ensure that the controller is compatible with the rest of the system hardware. Additionally, hardware RAID controllers with battery-backed cache can help protect data during power outages, preventing potential data loss from uncommitted transactions.

Physical damage to the RAID disks themselves is another significant failure mode. Disks, particularly hard disk drives (HDDs), are mechanical devices that are subject to wear and tear over time. Factors such as temperature fluctuations, vibrations, and excessive workloads can accelerate the degradation of disks, leading to sector errors, slow performance, or even complete failure. Even solid-state drives (SSDs), which have no moving parts, are not immune to failure. While SSDs offer higher performance and lower failure rates compared to HDDs, they are still subject to wear due to the limited number of write cycles that NAND flash memory can endure. To prevent physical damage to disks, RAID systems should be configured with proper environmental controls, such as adequate cooling, stable power supply, and vibration-free environments. Monitoring tools that track disk health, such as S.M.A.R.T. (Self-Monitoring, Analysis, and Reporting Technology), can alert administrators to signs of impending failure, allowing for proactive replacement before a complete disk failure occurs.

Another potential failure mode is data corruption within the RAID array. Data corruption can occur at various stages of the data lifecycle, whether during data entry, storage, or retrieval. In RAID systems, data corruption may happen due to software bugs, network issues, or even power failures during write operations. While RAID provides redundancy through parity or mirroring, corrupted data may still be replicated across multiple drives in the array, especially in the case of

RAID 1 or RAID 5 configurations. This can make it difficult to detect data corruption until the corrupted data is accessed, and recovery options may be limited. To mitigate the risk of data corruption, RAID systems should be integrated with error detection and correction mechanisms, such as error-correcting codes (ECC) or checksums, which can identify and correct minor data inconsistencies before they propagate. Furthermore, implementing regular data integrity checks, such as RAID consistency checks, can help detect issues early and prevent data corruption from spreading undetected.

Another failure mode that can occur in RAID systems is the failure during the rebuilding process. When a failed drive is replaced, the RAID array must rebuild the data onto the new drive using either mirrored data (in the case of RAID 1) or parity data (in the case of RAID 5 or RAID 6). During this rebuild process, the array is in a vulnerable state, and if another drive fails during this time, data loss can occur. Rebuild failures can be caused by a variety of factors, including insufficient disk space, hardware incompatibilities, or data inconsistencies. To reduce the risk of rebuild failures, it is essential to monitor the rebuild process closely and ensure that the new disk is properly integrated into the RAID array. Additionally, using a hot spare drive that is automatically used to replace a failed drive can help reduce downtime and speed up the rebuild process, minimizing the time the system operates in a degraded state.

Preventing RAID failures requires a proactive approach to both hardware and software management. Regular maintenance is key to preventing many of the failure modes discussed above. This includes routine monitoring of RAID arrays, firmware and software updates, and the replacement of aging hardware before failure occurs. Many RAID management systems offer monitoring tools that provide real-time information on the health of the array, including individual drive status, temperature readings, and error logs. Administrators should regularly check these logs for signs of potential issues and take corrective action before they lead to failure. Additionally, implementing automated error detection and recovery systems, such as RAID consistency checks and parity validation, can help catch and correct problems before they result in data loss.

A crucial aspect of RAID failure prevention is maintaining a reliable backup strategy. While RAID provides redundancy and fault tolerance, it cannot protect against every possible failure, such as catastrophic events, accidental deletion, or cyberattacks. Backups ensure that even if a RAID system fails completely, a copy of the data is available for recovery. Enterprises should implement a robust backup strategy that includes offsite or cloud-based backups, ensuring that data is protected from physical damage, theft, or disasters. Regular backup testing and verification ensure that the backup system works properly when it is needed most.

RAID systems, while reliable and efficient, are not infallible. Hardware failures, logical errors, and data corruption can all occur, threatening the integrity of the stored data. By understanding the various failure modes that RAID systems are susceptible to and implementing appropriate prevention strategies—such as regular maintenance, proactive disk monitoring, error detection and correction mechanisms, and robust backup solutions—organizations can ensure that their RAID systems continue to deliver the high levels of performance, availability, and reliability required to meet their growing data needs. By taking a comprehensive approach to RAID management and failure prevention, businesses can minimize the risk of data loss and ensure that their critical data remains protected at all times.

RAID in Remote Data Centers

Remote data centers have become increasingly vital in the modern digital world, providing essential services such as data storage, cloud computing, and hosting for businesses around the globe. As organizations continue to generate and rely on large volumes of data, maintaining high availability, performance, and reliability in remote data centers is critical. One technology that plays a fundamental role in achieving these goals is RAID (Redundant Array of Independent Disks). RAID provides redundancy, fault tolerance, and performance optimization by utilizing multiple hard drives or solid-state drives in an array. In remote data centers, where uptime is crucial and the risk of data loss can be devastating, RAID systems offer a robust solution to ensure that data is available even in the event of hardware failures.

The role of RAID in remote data centers can be best understood through its ability to provide fault tolerance. In a data center environment, a failure of a single disk could result in data loss, affecting the entire operation. This risk is exacerbated when data centers host critical applications, large-scale databases, or massive cloud storage solutions. RAID mitigates this risk by duplicating data across multiple disks, using either mirroring or parity, depending on the configuration. For instance, in RAID 1, data is mirrored across two or more disks, meaning that if one disk fails, the data is still available on the other disk. RAID 5 and RAID 6 extend this concept by combining striping with parity, allowing for data recovery even if one or two drives fail. This redundancy ensures that remote data centers can continue operating without service interruptions, even in the face of hardware failures.

In remote data centers, where data storage needs are often vast, RAID configurations such as RAID 5 or RAID 6 are particularly effective. These RAID levels provide an optimal balance between redundancy and storage efficiency, making them ideal for environments that require large-scale storage with high availability. RAID 5 distributes data across multiple disks and uses parity data to protect against single drive failures. The parity information allows the RAID system to rebuild lost data in the event of a failure. RAID 6 takes this a step further, adding an additional layer of protection by using double parity, which allows it to tolerate the failure of two drives simultaneously. These configurations provide both performance and redundancy, making them suitable for the diverse and demanding requirements of remote data centers.

Despite their advantages, RAID configurations, particularly those using parity, can introduce performance bottlenecks, especially in write-intensive environments. The need to calculate and update parity data during write operations can slow down overall performance, particularly in large-scale systems that experience frequent data writes. To address this issue, remote data centers may use SSDs (Solid-State Drives) in conjunction with RAID to improve performance. SSDs offer faster read and write speeds than traditional hard disk drives (HDDs), significantly reducing latency and improving throughput. By incorporating SSDs into RAID configurations, remote data centers can achieve both high performance and redundancy, ensuring that mission-critical applications and workloads continue to run smoothly.

Another challenge that RAID systems face in remote data centers is managing the scalability of storage systems. As data storage needs grow, RAID systems must be able to scale efficiently to accommodate increasing amounts of data. This scalability is essential in remote data centers, where the volume of data generated by clients or applications can grow exponentially over time. Many modern RAID systems are designed with scalability in mind, allowing data center operators to expand storage capacity by adding additional drives or even expanding the RAID array. This flexibility ensures that storage systems can keep pace with growing data requirements without significant disruptions to operations. Moreover, storage virtualization technologies are often used in remote data centers to further enhance scalability. These technologies abstract the underlying physical storage hardware and present a unified storage pool to the applications and servers. By combining RAID with storage virtualization, remote data centers can manage massive amounts of data more effectively, providing flexible and scalable storage solutions to meet the dynamic needs of their clients.

One key benefit of RAID in remote data centers is its ability to support high availability, ensuring that services remain operational even during hardware failures or maintenance. High availability is critical in remote data centers, where clients depend on constant access to their data and applications. RAID systems enable data center administrators to implement maintenance strategies that minimize downtime, such as hot swapping of drives. Hot swapping allows administrators to replace failed drives without interrupting service, ensuring that the data center remains operational while the system rebuilds the RAID array. Furthermore, RAID can be integrated with other high-availability technologies, such as load balancing and failover systems, to create a highly resilient infrastructure that minimizes the risk of service disruption.

Security is another critical concern in remote data centers, where sensitive data must be protected from unauthorized access, corruption, or loss. RAID alone cannot provide complete protection against data breaches or cyberattacks, but when combined with other security measures, it forms an essential part of a comprehensive data protection strategy. For example, RAID can be used in conjunction with encryption technologies to protect data both at rest and in transit. Encryption ensures that even if an attacker gains access to the storage array, the data remains unreadable without the appropriate decryption keys. Additionally, access control mechanisms can be implemented to limit who can interact with the RAID arrays, ensuring that only authorized personnel have access to critical data.

RAID systems in remote data centers also need to address the issue of disaster recovery. Data loss due to natural disasters, equipment failures, or human error can have catastrophic consequences for businesses. While RAID provides fault tolerance for disk failures, it cannot protect against large-scale disasters, such as fires, floods, or earthquakes, that may affect an entire data center. To mitigate this risk, remote data centers often implement disaster recovery strategies that include data replication and offsite backups. By replicating data across multiple geographic locations, remote data centers ensure that even if one site experiences a failure, the data remains accessible from another location. RAID-based replication solutions can be used to synchronize data between data centers, allowing for seamless data recovery in the event of a disaster.

Maintaining RAID systems in remote data centers requires careful planning, monitoring, and maintenance. RAID arrays should be continuously monitored to detect potential issues before they escalate into major problems. Modern RAID management tools provide real-time monitoring of the array's health, alerting administrators to issues such as failing drives, degraded performance, or inconsistencies in the data. Additionally, proactive maintenance practices, such as regular consistency checks, firmware updates, and drive replacements, help ensure that the RAID system continues to perform optimally over time.

RAID technology is an integral part of ensuring the reliability, availability, and performance of storage systems in remote data centers. By providing fault tolerance, performance optimization, and scalability, RAID helps data centers meet the growing demands of modern data-driven environments. When combined with other technologies such as SSDs, storage virtualization, encryption, and disaster recovery strategies, RAID enables remote data centers to deliver high-quality services to their clients while safeguarding data and minimizing downtime. As businesses continue to rely on remote data centers for mission-critical applications, the role of RAID in maintaining secure, resilient, and efficient storage systems will remain essential.

Understanding RAID and Its Impact on Data Availability

In today's digital landscape, data is the backbone of most businesses, institutions, and organizations, and its availability is crucial for operations. RAID (Redundant Array of Independent Disks) plays a key role in ensuring that data remains accessible even in the face of hardware failures. At its core, RAID is a technology that combines multiple physical hard drives or solid-state drives into a single, logical unit in order to improve the reliability, availability, and performance of data storage systems. With RAID, organizations can protect themselves against the risk of losing critical data while maintaining the high performance needed to support day-to-day operations. However, while RAID improves data availability by providing redundancy, it is important to understand both its benefits and limitations when considering it as a strategy for ensuring continuous access to data.

Data availability refers to the ability to access data whenever it is needed without disruption. In many critical environments, such as finance, healthcare, and e-commerce, even a few minutes of downtime can lead to substantial losses, whether in terms of revenue, customer trust, or operational efficiency. RAID, in its various configurations, is specifically designed to address the challenges of maintaining data availability. By distributing data across multiple disks and implementing mechanisms for redundancy, RAID systems can continue functioning even if one or more drives fail. The fundamental appeal of RAID lies in its ability to keep systems operational and data available in the event of hardware malfunctions, offering a safeguard against the single points of failure that occur with individual disks.

One of the most important factors to understand when discussing RAID and its impact on data availability is how different RAID levels provide varying degrees of redundancy and fault tolerance. For example, RAID 1, which mirrors data across two or more drives, ensures that if one drive fails, the data is still available from the mirrored drive. This makes RAID 1 highly effective for environments where reliability is crucial, and the data being handled is of high importance. However, the drawback of RAID 1 is that it requires twice the amount of storage since data is duplicated on multiple disks, making it less efficient in terms of capacity. While it provides excellent redundancy, the storage overhead is a significant factor to consider in environments where storage space is at a premium.

RAID 5 and RAID 6 are more commonly used in enterprise environments that require a balance between data protection and storage efficiency. RAID 5 uses a combination of striping and parity, where data is spread across multiple drives, and parity information is stored on one drive per block of data. In the event of a drive failure, the data can be rebuilt using the parity information, ensuring that the array remains operational with no data loss. RAID 5 can tolerate the failure of one drive, but it is vulnerable to further failures until the system has been rebuilt. RAID 6 improves upon RAID 5 by adding an additional layer of parity, allowing it to tolerate the failure of two drives. RAID 6 is particularly useful in large data centers or environments where the risk of multiple drive failures is higher, offering greater fault tolerance while still maintaining efficient use of storage.

The impact of RAID on data availability extends beyond just drive failures; it also addresses the issue of system performance. RAID configurations like RAID 0, which stripes data across multiple drives without redundancy, can significantly increase performance by enabling parallel data access. While RAID 0 offers no redundancy or protection against drive failure, its speed benefits are critical in environments where performance is a higher priority than data protection, such as in temporary data storage or applications requiring extremely high throughput. However, even in such cases, RAID 0's lack of fault tolerance is a serious limitation, as any single drive failure would result in complete data loss. This makes RAID 0 unsuitable for environments where data availability is essential.

RAID 10, which combines the mirroring of RAID 1 with the striping of RAID 0, is a powerful solution for applications that require both high availability and high performance. RAID 10 provides the redundancy of RAID 1, ensuring that data is mirrored across multiple disks, while also offering the speed of RAID 0 through striping. RAID 10 is particularly useful for high-transactional environments, such as database systems, where both speed and data integrity are paramount. However, like RAID 1, RAID 10 incurs the cost of requiring twice the storage capacity of the data being stored due to the mirroring aspect. Despite the storage inefficiency, the combination of performance and redundancy that RAID 10 offers makes it one of the most reliable RAID configurations for enterprise environments.

While RAID provides significant improvements in data availability, it is important to remember that it is not a comprehensive data protection solution. RAID protects against hardware failures by providing redundancy, but it does not safeguard against other types of data loss, such as corruption due to software bugs, human error, ransomware, or malicious attacks. For instance, if data becomes corrupted or deleted, RAID will replicate the corrupted or deleted data across the array, rendering recovery impossible without an external backup. This is why RAID should be part of a larger data protection strategy that includes regular backups, disaster recovery plans, and security measures to safeguard data from various types of risks.

RAID can also have an impact on the overall reliability and performance of a system depending on how it is configured and managed. While RAID 5 and RAID 6 are excellent for providing fault tolerance and efficient storage, they come with the overhead of parity calculations, which can introduce latency, particularly in write-intensive operations. In some cases, the performance of RAID 5 or RAID 6 might be slower than that of RAID 1 or RAID 10, especially during the rebuild process, when the system must recalculate and reconstruct data from the remaining drives. This performance impact is something that must be considered when choosing the appropriate RAID level for an environment where both high availability and performance are essential.

Managing RAID in large-scale environments, particularly in remote or distributed data centers, also requires careful planning to ensure that data availability is maintained. Remote data centers often operate with a variety of RAID configurations to meet the diverse needs of different applications, and maintaining consistency and high availability across multiple RAID arrays can be challenging. This is especially true when RAID arrays are spread across multiple physical locations, requiring complex management tools and monitoring systems to ensure that all systems are operating optimally. Additionally, remote data centers must have robust backup strategies in place to ensure that RAID is complemented by a secondary form of data protection, such as cloud backups or offsite replication, to provide a full-fledged disaster recovery plan.

RAID has a significant impact on data availability by improving fault tolerance, providing redundancy, and enhancing system performance. While it is not a complete solution for every data protection challenge, it is a critical component in ensuring that data remains accessible in the event of hardware failures. Whether through RAID 1's mirroring, RAID 5's parity, or RAID 10's combination of both redundancy and performance, RAID systems offer the ability to maintain data availability in environments that require uninterrupted access to data. As organizations continue to generate and rely on increasingly large amounts of data, RAID remains an indispensable tool in ensuring the resilience and accessibility of that data, making it a cornerstone of modern data storage strategies.

Legal and Compliance Considerations in RAID Configurations

As businesses and organizations increasingly rely on data for decision-making, operations, and customer interactions, the importance of maintaining data integrity, availability, and security cannot be overstated. RAID (Redundant Array of Independent Disks) configurations are essential tools in protecting against data loss, providing fault tolerance, and improving the performance of storage systems. However, as organizations store more sensitive and critical information, they must also be mindful of legal and compliance considerations related to data storage and management. These considerations play a crucial role in ensuring that RAID configurations meet the regulatory requirements set forth by various industries and governments to protect data privacy and security. Understanding the intersection of RAID technology with legal and compliance frameworks is essential for businesses looking to balance performance and security in their data storage systems.

RAID systems are primarily used to enhance data redundancy, ensuring that even in the event of hardware failures, data remains available. This functionality is essential in industries that handle sensitive information, such as healthcare, finance, and government. For example, RAID's ability to maintain data availability during hardware failures is particularly relevant in compliance-heavy sectors like healthcare, where regulations such as HIPAA (Health Insurance Portability and Accountability Act) mandate strict data availability and privacy standards. In these industries, RAID configurations must be designed and managed in a way that ensures data is not only protected from physical failure but also secured against unauthorized access, breaches, or tampering.

In addition to ensuring that data is available, compliance regulations often impose strict data protection requirements. For example, the GDPR (General Data Protection Regulation) in the European Union requires that organizations implement appropriate technical and organizational measures to protect personal data. RAID configurations, by providing redundancy and protecting against hardware failures, are often seen as one aspect of ensuring compliance with such regulations. However, RAID alone does not address the full scope of data protection requirements. For instance, while RAID may protect against hardware failures, it does not inherently provide encryption or prevent unauthorized access to the data. As a result, organizations must implement additional security measures, such as encryption and access controls, to comply with legal requirements that safeguard personal or sensitive data.

One of the key legal and compliance challenges associated with RAID configurations is ensuring the proper handling and storage of personal data. Many regulations, including GDPR and CCPA (California Consumer Privacy Act), require organizations to store personal data securely and to ensure that this data is accessible only to authorized individuals. RAID, particularly when configured with mirrored or striped data, can improve data availability and redundancy, but it does not provide the mechanisms necessary to protect the confidentiality and integrity of personal data. For example, organizations must ensure that RAID arrays are configured in a manner that prevents unauthorized access, including protecting data stored in unencrypted drives. RAID administrators should incorporate encryption technologies into RAID configurations, ensuring that data is encrypted both at rest and in transit. This helps prevent unauthorized parties from accessing sensitive information, especially if the storage devices are physically stolen or compromised.

Another key compliance issue that organizations must consider when implementing RAID configurations is the retention and deletion of data. Many legal and regulatory frameworks require organizations to retain data for a specific period, after which it must be deleted or anonymized. RAID systems, by their very nature, are designed to store large volumes of data with redundancy, which can present challenges when organizations must comply with regulations that mandate the deletion of certain types of data after a set retention period. For instance, GDPR mandates that personal data be stored no longer than necessary for the purposes for which it was collected. RAID configurations that do not incorporate proper data management policies could lead to the inadvertent retention of data beyond the required period, violating compliance requirements. To mitigate this, organizations need to implement clear data retention and deletion policies, incorporating RAID systems into their data lifecycle management strategies to ensure that data is disposed of in a manner that complies with legal requirements.

RAID also plays a role in maintaining business continuity, which is often a key component of compliance regulations. In industries such as finance or government, where operational downtime can result in significant financial losses or regulatory penalties, RAID systems ensure that data remains available even in the event of hardware failures. For instance, in financial institutions, compliance with regulations such as SOX (Sarbanes-Oxley Act) mandates that organizations maintain accurate records and ensure the availability of financial data for audit purposes. RAID systems help maintain this level of availability by offering redundancy through mirroring, striping, or parity, ensuring that data can be recovered or accessed in case of drive failure. However, organizations must also ensure that the RAID systems are continuously monitored and maintained to prevent data loss during system rebuilds or other maintenance activities. This is particularly important when operating in remote or distributed data centers, where the risk of equipment failure may be higher.

Auditability is another critical consideration in compliance requirements, particularly in industries with stringent regulations like banking, healthcare, and government. RAID systems must be designed to allow organizations to audit and track data access, modifications, and deletions. Compliance regulations often require that organizations maintain comprehensive logs that record who accessed data, when, and what changes were made. In the context of RAID configurations, this means that administrators must ensure that RAID systems are integrated with centralized logging and monitoring tools that capture these access patterns. This auditability ensures that organizations can prove compliance in the event of a regulatory inspection or audit, reducing the risk of non-compliance penalties.

The physical location of RAID storage systems also has legal and compliance implications, especially for organizations that operate internationally. Various regulations, such as GDPR and CCPA, impose restrictions on where data can be stored and processed, particularly when it involves personal or sensitive information. For example, GDPR imposes restrictions on transferring personal data outside the EU to countries that do not have an adequate level of data protection. RAID systems that span multiple geographic locations must ensure that data is stored in compliance with these regulations, which may require localizing data storage or using encryption techniques to ensure that sensitive data remains protected during transfers.

RAID systems, particularly in the context of large-scale deployments like cloud environments or distributed networks, must also comply with security measures like vulnerability management, patching, and system hardening. Compliance regulations often require that data storage systems are protected against known vulnerabilities and are updated regularly to address security flaws. RAID configurations, being part of the broader storage infrastructure, must be regularly maintained and patched to ensure that they are not exposed to security risks that could lead to data breaches or loss.

RAID configurations have a significant impact on data availability, redundancy, and performance, but they must also be designed and managed with legal and compliance considerations in mind. Data protection laws and regulations demand that organizations not only secure their data against hardware failures but also protect its confidentiality, integrity, and accessibility. By integrating encryption, access controls, and proper data retention policies, organizations can ensure that their RAID systems comply with the various legal and regulatory frameworks that govern data privacy and security. RAID systems are a powerful tool for improving data availability and reducing the risk of data loss, but they must be part of a broader strategy that encompasses all aspects of data protection and regulatory compliance.

Troubleshooting Common RAID Issues

RAID (Redundant Array of Independent Disks) is an essential technology used in data storage to provide redundancy, improve performance, and enhance data availability. While RAID can be incredibly reliable when configured correctly, it is not without its challenges. As with any technology, RAID arrays can encounter issues that affect their performance, reliability, and the accessibility of data. Troubleshooting RAID problems can be complex, especially in large-scale environments where multiple drives, controllers, and configurations are in use. Understanding the common issues that arise with RAID arrays and knowing how to address them is essential for maintaining optimal system performance and ensuring that data remains available in case of failure.

One of the most common issues encountered in RAID systems is drive failure. While RAID is designed to protect against single drive failures, it is not immune to them. When a drive fails in a RAID 1, RAID 5, or RAID 6 configuration, the system continues to operate in a degraded mode, but it becomes vulnerable to additional drive failures. The first step in troubleshooting this issue is to identify the failed drive. Many

RAID systems and RAID controllers provide monitoring tools that alert administrators when a drive has failed. These tools often use indicators such as LED lights on the drives or error messages in the RAID management interface to point out which drive has failed. Once the failed drive is identified, the next step is to replace the drive with a new one of the same size or larger, depending on the RAID level. In the case of RAID 5 or RAID 6, the array will rebuild itself using the remaining drives and parity data. It is crucial to monitor the rebuild process to ensure it completes successfully, as a second drive failure during the rebuild can result in data loss.

Another common RAID issue is data inconsistency or corruption, which can occur during a rebuild process, after a power outage, or as a result of system crashes. In RAID systems that use parity, such as RAID 5 or RAID 6, the parity data is crucial for rebuilding lost data in case of a drive failure. However, if there is an issue with the parity data or if the rebuild process is interrupted, data inconsistency can occur. In some cases, the RAID system may flag the array as degraded, but data may still be accessible. However, inconsistent data could lead to corruption or, in the worst-case scenario, data loss. Troubleshooting this problem involves checking the integrity of the RAID array and verifying the parity information. Many RAID management tools offer consistency check features, which can scan the array for inconsistencies between the data and the parity information. If inconsistencies are found, the system will attempt to correct them. It is essential to back up the data as soon as possible to avoid further issues.

RAID 0, which stripes data across multiple drives without redundancy, is another configuration that is prone to issues when a drive fails. Since there is no mirroring or parity in RAID 0, a single drive failure results in the complete loss of all data stored on the array. One of the challenges in troubleshooting RAID 0 failures is the inability to rebuild the array. If one drive in a RAID 0 array fails, there is no way to recover the lost data unless it has been backed up elsewhere. The best strategy for troubleshooting RAID 0 issues is to ensure that backups are performed regularly to prevent permanent data loss in the event of drive failure. In cases where the data on a failed RAID 0 array must be recovered, data recovery services may be required, but these services can be expensive and are not always guaranteed to work.

Another issue that can affect RAID systems is controller failure. The RAID controller is responsible for managing the data flow between the drives and ensuring that the RAID configuration operates correctly. If the controller fails, the entire RAID array may become inaccessible, even if the drives themselves are still functioning correctly. Troubleshooting controller issues involves several steps, starting with checking the physical connections, including the cables and power supply, to ensure there are no loose connections. Next, the administrator should check the controller's firmware to ensure it is up to date, as outdated firmware can cause compatibility issues or bugs. If the controller is faulty, replacing it with a new one that is compatible with the existing RAID configuration is necessary. It is also important to ensure that the RAID configuration is backed up before replacing the controller, as some controllers may not be able to read the array properly after being swapped out.

Another common issue in RAID systems is performance degradation. RAID configurations, particularly those that involve parity calculations like RAID 5 or RAID 6, can experience a decrease in performance, especially in write-heavy environments. Parity calculations can add overhead to the system, slowing down write speeds. This is particularly noticeable during a rebuild process, where the RAID array must recalculate parity information for the entire array. If performance degradation is observed, troubleshooting should start with checking the system's CPU and memory usage to ensure there is enough processing power to handle the parity calculations. In some cases, upgrading the RAID controller to one with a higher processing capacity or adding additional cache memory to the system can help alleviate the performance bottleneck. Additionally, using faster disks, such as SSDs, in place of slower HDDs can significantly improve the overall performance of the RAID array.

Additionally, RAID configurations may experience issues with disk misalignment, which can occur when partitions on the disks are not aligned with the RAID array's striping scheme. This misalignment can lead to inefficient read and write operations, negatively affecting performance. Disk misalignment is particularly common when migrating from older systems or when using SSDs with RAID arrays. Troubleshooting this issue involves realigning the disk partitions to match the RAID array's striping configuration. Many modern RAID management tools provide features to check and correct disk alignment, which can help restore optimal performance.

Over time, RAID arrays can become fragmented, especially in environments where data is constantly being written and deleted. Fragmentation occurs when data is spread across multiple disks in a non-contiguous manner, leading to slower read and write speeds. While RAID itself does not cause fragmentation, it can exacerbate performance issues if not properly maintained. The best way to troubleshoot fragmentation issues is to regularly monitor disk health and performance. In some cases, defragmenting the RAID array can improve performance, although this is more relevant for HDD-based RAID systems. For SSD-based RAID systems, fragmentation is less of an issue due to the way SSDs handle data storage, but periodic system checks and optimizations should still be conducted.

Lastly, RAID systems in large-scale environments may encounter issues related to the sheer scale of the deployment. For example, RAID arrays consisting of hundreds of drives may suffer from issues such as disk sprawl or imbalanced storage utilization, which can lead to inefficiencies and slower performance. Troubleshooting these issues requires monitoring the storage usage across all drives and redistributing data across the array to ensure that no individual disk is overburdened. Implementing tiered storage, where data is placed on different types of storage devices based on usage, can also help optimize performance in large-scale RAID environments.

RAID arrays are powerful tools for ensuring data availability and reliability, but they are not immune to issues that can compromise performance and data integrity. Troubleshooting common RAID issues involves a combination of monitoring, regular maintenance, and timely replacement of faulty components. By understanding the typical failure modes and performance bottlenecks associated with RAID systems, administrators can implement strategies to mitigate these issues, ensuring that RAID configurations continue to deliver the performance and redundancy necessary to meet the needs of modern storage environments.

RAID for Home and Small Business Use

In an era where data plays a central role in both personal and professional life, ensuring that data is stored safely and remains accessible is crucial. For home users and small businesses, data protection is often just as important as for large enterprises, albeit with different constraints on budgets, resources, and expertise. RAID (Redundant Array of Independent Disks) technology, traditionally used in large-scale enterprise environments, has become an increasingly viable solution for home and small business use. By combining multiple hard drives or solid-state drives into a single logical unit, RAID provides redundancy, performance optimization, and enhanced data availability, offering a level of protection against hardware failures that is necessary for safeguarding critical information.

Home users and small businesses face unique challenges when it comes to data management. In a typical home environment, users store everything from family photos to important documents and videos. Small businesses, on the other hand, rely on digital storage for everything from customer records to financial data and operational documents. While cloud services have become a popular backup and storage option, many people prefer the security and control of local storage, which is where RAID comes into play. RAID can offer home users and small businesses a cost-effective solution for improving both the speed and reliability of their data storage.

For home users, the most straightforward and affordable RAID configurations, such as RAID 1 (mirroring), are ideal. RAID 1 provides redundancy by duplicating data across two or more drives. This means that if one drive fails, the data remains accessible from the other drive. Given the typically smaller storage needs of home users, RAID 1 strikes a balance between data protection and affordability, providing peace of mind for those who store valuable photos, videos, and personal documents on their home computers or network-attached storage (NAS) devices. By offering an additional layer of security, RAID 1 can protect against the kind of data loss that occurs due to the failure of a single hard drive.

Small businesses, which often store larger volumes of data, may require more advanced RAID configurations like RAID 5 or RAID 10. RAID 5 combines striping and parity, distributing data across multiple drives with parity information, allowing for data recovery in the event of a single drive failure. RAID 5 is often chosen by small businesses due to its cost-effectiveness, as it allows for fault tolerance while maintaining storage efficiency. In a small business environment, RAID 5 can be used to store critical operational data and customer information, ensuring that business continuity is maintained even in the face of hardware failures.

RAID 10, which combines the redundancy of RAID 1 with the performance benefits of RAID 0 (striping), is another popular option for small businesses. RAID 10 provides a balance of high performance and redundancy, making it ideal for environments where both speed and data protection are important. This RAID configuration offers excellent fault tolerance, as it mirrors data across multiple drives while also improving read and write speeds by distributing the data across multiple disks. For small businesses that run applications requiring high-speed data access, such as database systems or file-sharing services, RAID 10 is an attractive option, although it comes at the expense of storage efficiency, as it requires twice the number of drives to store the data.

While RAID offers clear advantages in terms of data protection and performance, home users and small businesses must also be aware of the associated complexities and costs. One of the key challenges is the initial setup and ongoing management of RAID systems. For small businesses, managing RAID arrays, monitoring the health of drives, and ensuring proper configuration can require some level of technical expertise. Fortunately, many consumer-grade RAID systems, such as those built into NAS devices or external RAID enclosures, provide user-friendly management interfaces that allow non-technical users to set up and manage RAID without needing specialized knowledge. Home users can also take advantage of these easy-to-use systems, which allow them to protect their personal data without complex configurations.

Another challenge for home users and small businesses is the cost of implementing RAID. While RAID offers significant benefits in terms of data protection, it requires multiple hard drives or SSDs to be effective, and this can add up in terms of cost. For home users, RAID 1 may be a suitable solution because it only requires two drives, making it relatively affordable. For small businesses, RAID 5 or RAID 10 requires a larger number of drives, which can significantly increase the initial investment. However, the cost of RAID can be offset by the potential savings in terms of data recovery. In a small business, the loss of critical data can result in lost revenue, legal ramifications, and damage to the company's reputation, making the investment in a reliable RAID system a wise decision.

Moreover, the performance of RAID can be impacted by the type of drives used in the configuration. While HDDs (Hard Disk Drives) have traditionally been used in RAID systems, SSDs (Solid-State Drives) are increasingly being integrated into RAID configurations for their speed and durability. For home users and small businesses looking to improve their system performance, investing in SSD-based RAID configurations can offer substantial improvements in terms of speed, particularly for applications that involve large data sets or require high throughput, such as video editing or virtualization. However, SSDs are typically more expensive than HDDs, and the cost can be a barrier for smaller setups, especially for home users.

In a home environment, RAID is most commonly used in NAS devices, which offer centralized storage that can be accessed by multiple devices within the home. These NAS units can be configured with RAID for data redundancy and performance optimization, providing a secure storage solution for families who need to store large amounts of data across different devices, such as computers, smartphones, and tablets. Small businesses may also use RAID in NAS or SAN (Storage Area Network) solutions, providing centralized, secure, and high-performance data storage that can be shared across multiple employees or departments.

Another key consideration for home users and small businesses implementing RAID is the need for regular backups. While RAID provides redundancy, it does not protect against all forms of data loss, such as user error, malware attacks, or corruption. For home users, implementing a reliable backup strategy alongside RAID is essential to ensure that data can be recovered in case of accidental deletion or system failure. Small businesses must also implement off-site or cloud-based backups in addition to RAID configurations, ensuring that critical data is protected against disasters such as fires, floods, or theft. Regular backup practices complement the protection offered by RAID, providing an additional layer of data security.

RAID technology provides home users and small businesses with a powerful tool to ensure the reliability, availability, and protection of their data. By choosing the appropriate RAID level, users can balance the trade-offs between data redundancy, performance, and cost. While RAID can help mitigate the risk of data loss due to hardware failures, it should be combined with other data protection strategies, such as regular backups, to create a comprehensive data security plan. For both home users and small businesses, RAID offers a viable and cost-effective solution to ensure that their critical data is safe, accessible, and protected from failure.

The Cost of RAID: Financial Considerations

RAID (Redundant Array of Independent Disks) is a technology that has become essential in modern data storage, offering solutions that provide redundancy, increased performance, and data integrity. By using multiple hard drives or solid-state drives in a single logical unit, RAID configurations help protect data from hardware failure while also improving the speed of data access. However, the implementation of RAID comes with its own set of financial considerations, especially when used in enterprise environments, small businesses, or even personal setups. The costs associated with RAID can vary depending on the configuration, the hardware used, and the level of redundancy required. It is important to understand these costs before deciding to adopt RAID, as the financial implications can impact an organization's overall IT budget and storage strategy.

One of the primary costs associated with RAID is the price of the hard drives or solid-state drives that make up the array. Unlike traditional single-drive systems, RAID requires multiple drives, which significantly increases the initial investment. For example, in a basic RAID 1 setup, two hard drives are required to mirror data. The cost of these drives can vary depending on the size, type, and performance characteristics of the drives. A high-performance setup using SSDs (Solid-State Drives) can be considerably more expensive than one using traditional HDDs (Hard Disk Drives), especially when scaling up to larger arrays. The larger the capacity and the more advanced the RAID level, such as RAID 10, RAID 5, or RAID 6, the more drives will be required, driving up the costs even further. While SSDs provide faster speeds and improved reliability compared to HDDs, their higher upfront cost can be prohibitive for some organizations, especially small businesses or home users looking for a cost-effective storage solution.

Beyond the cost of the individual drives themselves, RAID systems also require specialized hardware, such as RAID controllers, to manage the data flow between the drives and maintain the integrity of the RAID array. RAID controllers are responsible for overseeing the storage configuration, ensuring data is correctly striped, mirrored, or parity-protected across the disks. These controllers are often equipped with built-in cache memory and advanced features to manage large arrays, improve performance, and handle drive failures. While basic RAID controller cards for home or small business use may be relatively affordable, enterprise-level RAID controllers with advanced features like battery backup, high throughput, and support for larger arrays can be quite expensive. Depending on the RAID level and the specific needs of the system, the cost of RAID controllers can be a substantial part of the overall financial investment in a RAID-based storage solution.

Another important financial consideration when implementing RAID is the cost of redundancy. While redundancy is a primary advantage of RAID, it comes at the cost of storage efficiency. For instance, in a RAID 1 setup, data is mirrored across two drives, meaning that only half of the total storage capacity is usable. In RAID 5 or RAID 6, parity is distributed across multiple drives to provide fault tolerance, but this also means that part of the storage capacity is reserved for parity data. In these configurations, although the system offers redundancy and fault tolerance, the total usable storage is reduced, which means additional drives are required to meet the same storage needs. As a result, organizations need to carefully consider their storage requirements and balance the benefits of redundancy against the additional cost of the drives needed to maintain the system.

For businesses, one of the hidden costs of RAID can be the operational and maintenance expenses associated with managing the storage system. RAID arrays require regular monitoring to ensure that the drives are functioning properly and that the data remains protected. As RAID systems become larger and more complex, so does the need for skilled IT staff to maintain the system, troubleshoot issues, and manage the health of the array. The costs of hiring or training personnel with the necessary expertise in RAID configurations and maintenance can add up over time. Additionally, businesses must plan for the ongoing cost of replacing failed drives, which can be costly depending on the RAID configuration and the type of drives used. Even with RAID's fault tolerance features, drives can still fail, and the process of replacing a failed drive and rebuilding the array can lead to downtime, which may affect business operations.

The cost of RAID systems also extends to the data protection strategy employed alongside RAID. While RAID offers redundancy and protection against hardware failures, it does not fully protect against other risks, such as accidental deletion, malware, or ransomware attacks. To fully protect data, businesses must incorporate additional backup strategies, such as off-site backups, cloud storage, or tape drives. These backup systems, while crucial for ensuring comprehensive data protection, come with their own costs. Cloud-based backup services, for example, often involve recurring monthly or yearly fees based on the amount of data being stored. Off-site backups can require significant infrastructure investments, including the cost of storing physical backup devices in secure locations. Additionally, backup strategies may require software licenses and maintenance fees to ensure the system is running smoothly. The added costs of these backup solutions must be considered when calculating the overall financial commitment to RAID-based storage.

For home users, the financial considerations of RAID are often simpler but still significant. Many home users opt for RAID 1 in personal NAS (Network-Attached Storage) devices to protect their personal data, such as photos, videos, and important documents. While RAID 1 provides data redundancy, it also requires two hard drives, effectively doubling the cost of storage. For users looking for higher performance, upgrading to SSDs for RAID arrays will further increase costs. For small businesses, the decision to implement RAID can become more complex, as their storage needs often grow over time, requiring larger arrays and more sophisticated RAID configurations. RAID 5 or RAID 10 may become more attractive options, but they come with the added cost of additional drives, RAID controllers, and backup systems.

Energy consumption is another ongoing cost associated with RAID systems. Although RAID configurations help with data management and redundancy, the number of drives in the array and the need for continuous operation can increase power consumption. In environments with large RAID arrays, the electricity costs to power multiple hard drives and RAID controllers can become significant. This is especially true in small businesses that run 24/7 operations and require high availability. For home users, energy consumption is typically less of an issue, but it still adds to the operational cost of running RAID systems in personal or home-office setups.

When considering the financial aspects of RAID, it is essential to weigh the costs against the potential benefits, such as improved data security, reliability, and performance. While RAID systems require a substantial upfront investment, the protection they offer against data loss and the increase in operational efficiency can provide significant returns over time. For businesses, the costs associated with RAID can be justified by the reduction in the risk of data loss, which could otherwise result in lost revenue, damaged reputation, or regulatory penalties. For home users, the decision to implement RAID is often driven by the desire to protect personal data and ensure the availability of important files.

Ultimately, the cost of RAID is a complex consideration that goes beyond the price of the hardware alone. It includes ongoing operational costs, maintenance expenses, backup strategies, and even energy consumption. For home users, small businesses, and large enterprises alike, RAID offers a powerful solution to improve data availability and protect against hardware failures, but it is essential to carefully plan and budget for the costs associated with its implementation and ongoing management.

Conclusion: The Ongoing Relevance of RAID in Data Storage Systems

As the demand for data storage continues to grow exponentially, the need for reliable, efficient, and secure storage solutions has never been more crucial. RAID (Redundant Array of Independent Disks) has long been a cornerstone of data storage systems, providing redundancy, performance optimization, and enhanced data availability. Despite the emergence of newer technologies such as cloud storage and software-defined storage, RAID remains an indispensable part of modern storage infrastructures, offering unique advantages that ensure data integrity, protection, and availability. The ongoing relevance of RAID in both personal and enterprise environments underscores its continued importance in the face of evolving technological landscapes and shifting data management needs.

One of the key factors driving the ongoing relevance of RAID is its ability to offer fault tolerance and redundancy. As organizations and individuals generate and store vast amounts of critical data, the risk of data loss due to hardware failure becomes an ever-present concern. RAID provides a reliable safeguard against these risks by distributing data across multiple disks and implementing redundancy mechanisms such as mirroring or parity. In RAID configurations like RAID 1, data is mirrored across two or more drives, ensuring that even if one drive fails, the data remains accessible. In other RAID levels such as RAID 5 and RAID 6, parity information is used to reconstruct data in the event of a failure. These redundancy features help maintain business continuity by minimizing downtime and ensuring that data is always available, even in the face of hardware malfunctions.

The importance of data availability has never been more pronounced than in today's fast-paced digital world, where downtime can lead to significant financial losses, reputational damage, and regulatory penalties. RAID systems, with their fault-tolerant architecture, provide a robust solution for businesses that require constant access to data. For instance, in industries such as healthcare, finance, and e-commerce, where real-time data processing and access are critical, RAID ensures that data remains available even during system maintenance or hardware failures. By providing a safety net against unexpected disruptions, RAID allows organizations to continue operating seamlessly, thus minimizing the risk of downtime and protecting vital business operations.

In addition to fault tolerance, RAID offers improved performance through various configurations. RAID 0, for example, enhances system performance by striping data across multiple disks, allowing for faster read and write speeds. This is particularly valuable in high-performance environments such as video editing, gaming, and data-intensive applications, where quick data access is paramount. While RAID 0 does not provide redundancy, its ability to boost performance makes it an attractive choice in scenarios where speed is more critical than data protection. More complex configurations like RAID 10, which combines the benefits of RAID 1 and RAID 0, offer both improved performance and redundancy, making it a popular choice in enterprise environments where high availability and fast data access are essential.

Despite the advantages of RAID, it is important to recognize its limitations and the changing landscape of data storage. Cloud storage and software-defined storage systems have risen in prominence in recent years, offering scalability, flexibility, and remote access capabilities that RAID does not inherently provide. Cloud storage, in particular, has become a go-to solution for many organizations and individuals due to its offsite redundancy and ease of access. However, even with the rise of cloud storage, RAID continues to offer unique benefits that cloud services cannot fully replicate, particularly in terms of local, high-performance storage for businesses and individuals who require on-premise solutions.

One of the most notable advantages of RAID over cloud storage is its control over the physical hardware. With RAID, users have complete control over their data storage infrastructure, allowing them to manage their systems in ways that are not possible with cloud providers. For businesses that handle sensitive or proprietary data, maintaining full control over their storage systems can be a significant advantage, as it ensures that data does not leave the premises or fall into the hands of third-party vendors. This level of control is particularly important for organizations that must comply with strict regulatory frameworks, such as GDPR, HIPAA, or SOC 2, which require that sensitive data be stored and accessed under specific conditions. RAID systems, when configured and managed properly, can meet these regulatory requirements by providing secure, high-performance, and fault-tolerant storage solutions that remain within the organization's control.

Another reason for RAID's ongoing relevance is the cost-effectiveness of certain RAID configurations. For small businesses and home users, implementing RAID can provide significant benefits without the need for costly cloud subscriptions or the complexities of managing large-scale storage infrastructures. Basic RAID configurations, such as RAID 1 for redundancy or RAID 5 for a balance of performance and fault tolerance, offer an affordable way to protect data while improving system performance. These RAID systems can be implemented using relatively inexpensive hardware, making them accessible to individuals and small businesses with limited IT budgets. As the price of storage devices continues to decrease, RAID remains a cost-effective option for those looking to protect their data while maintaining performance.

RAID is also evolving to meet the needs of modern data storage requirements. With the advent of SSDs (Solid-State Drives), RAID configurations that utilize SSDs are becoming increasingly popular due to their superior speed, durability, and reliability. SSDs offer much faster read and write speeds than traditional hard drives, making them ideal for high-performance RAID configurations that require quick data access. RAID systems that incorporate SSDs provide a significant boost in speed and performance, which is especially valuable in applications such as virtualization, big data processing, and real-time analytics. The continued improvement in SSD technology, along with the decreasing cost of SSDs, ensures that RAID will remain relevant in the era of high-performance storage.

As businesses continue to generate more data and the demand for data availability and protection grows, RAID will continue to be a crucial part of data storage strategies. Whether through local storage for businesses that require high-speed access and control over their data, or as part of a hybrid solution that incorporates both RAID and cloud storage, RAID remains a powerful tool for ensuring the integrity, performance, and redundancy of data storage systems. Even as newer technologies emerge, RAID's foundational benefits—data protection, performance optimization, and scalability—continue to make it a relevant and valuable solution for businesses and individuals alike. The flexibility and versatility of RAID, along with its ability to evolve in tandem with advancements in storage technology, ensure that it will remain a key player in the world of data storage for years to come.

www.ingramcontent.com/pod-product-compliance
Lightning Source LLC
Chambersburg PA
CBHW071153050326
40689CB00011B/2099